TABLE OF CONTENTS

DISCLAIMER AND TERMS OF USE AGREEMENT:

Introduction - Ready, Set: Write – Publish – Sell!

Chapter 1 - Optimization Techniques

Chapter 2 - Promotional Techniques

Chapter 3 - Good Ol' Fashion EMAIL MARKETING

Chapter 4 - Combination Marketing Techniques

Chapter 5 - Book Tours & Event Marketing Techniques

Chapter 6 - EPublishing Platforms Your Books Need To Be On

Chapter 7 - Audio Books

Chapter 8 - Automated Postcards

Chapter 9 - Books to TV

Chapter 10 - Fast TV Exposure

Chapter 11 - Appendix of Advertising & Marketing Resources

I Have a Special Gift for My Readers

Meet the Author

How to Promote Your Book Online & Offline
Online & Offline Techniques That Push Your Book to
Bestseller!
©Copyright 2013 by Dr. Leland Benton

DISCLAIMER AND TERMS OF USE AGREEMENT:

(Please Read This Before Using This Book)

This information is for educational and informational
purposes only. The content is not intended to be a
substitute for any professional advice, diagnosis, or
treatment.

The authors and publisher of this book and the
accompanying materials have used their best efforts in
preparing this book.

The authors and publisher make no representation or
warranties with respect to the accuracy, applicability,
fitness, or completeness of the contents of this book. The
information contained in this book is strictly for
educational purposes. Therefore, if you wish to apply

ideas contained in this book, you are taking full responsibility for your actions.

The authors and publisher disclaim any warranties (express or implied), merchantability, or fitness for any particular purpose. The author and publisher shall in no event be held liable to any party for any direct, indirect, punitive, special, incidental or other consequential damages arising directly or indirectly from any use of this material, which is provided "as is", and without warranties. As always, the advice of a competent legal, tax, accounting, medical or other professional should be sought where applicable.

The authors and publisher do not warrant the performance, effectiveness or applicability of any sites listed or linked to in this book. All links are for information purposes only and are not warranted for content, accuracy or any other implied or explicit purpose. No part of this may be copied, or changed in any format, or used in any way other than what is outlined within this course under any circumstances. Violators will be prosecuted.

Welcome to my world…and it is a very marvelous world, too. Because of ePublishing, I make over five figures per month, and this figure is just on Amazon alone. I have over 200 ebooks published, and the sum total I am published on is over two dozen platforms.

Kindle is hot, and you get it and I get it, but they aren't the only game in town. In this book, I will show you some of the other ePublishing platforms. This book describes everything I do within the realm of epublishing and is designed for self-publishing authors.

In my book, "Publish with a Purpose" I describe how to make money writing books for other people. This is just another way to monetize ePublishing.

Taking it another step further, in my book "How to Write a Kindle Book in Hours" I show people that can't even write a sentence how to become self-published.

Candidly, there is so much opportunity within the ePublishing realm; I have only included in this book the most lucrative ones.

This book is dedicated to promotion and advertising any ebook or printed book. I use all of the techniques described in this book. If you have any questions, please write to our support desk - mailto:support@epubwealth.com.

I have been publishing on Kindle since it began in 2007. Before that, Amazon only offered paperback and hard cover books, and this was even before CreateSpace, (which they own). For those of you unfamiliar with CreateSpace, this is Amazon's Print-On-Demand (POD) platform for paperback and hard cover physical books.

Last year (2011), my Kindle sales outpaced my CreateSpace sales, but Kindle isn't my best sales platform. My best platform is Smashwords. I sell more books through Smashwords than any other ePublishing platform. Interestingly enough, Kobo is fast becoming an ePublishing paradise. Don't worry; it is all in this book!

To me there are two types of authors – one who simply writes and publishes to make money and the second is one who writes to make a statement and make a difference.

Both are fine with me, and I do not judge, but I personally fall into the second category. Yes, I do like making money as an author, but I have a good amount of words inside of me aching to get out so making a statement and making a difference is important to me.

I write under a dozen different pen names and many genres. My company – ePubWealth.com – is an ePublisher where I have over a dozen staff writers whom we publish for as well as independent indie authors that rely on us to push their books into the marketplace using what I will describe herein.

Within my company's hierarchy, I wear many hats but the most rewarding and fulfilling is ePubWealth where I am Editor-in-Chief.

I have been a behavioral scientist and doctor for over 31-years, and I am also the Managing Director of Applied Mind Sciences, which is the research arm to our company where we conduct mind research and apply it commercially to advertising, human resources, law enforcement, and much more.

I am also the Chief Forensics Investigator for our ForensicsNation.com division where I created the software and programs to track down cyber-criminals, and we are very good at it, too.

As you can see, I have my hands in a good many pies but with each and every project I do I also write books about it, and this is how I make a difference and a statement.

Okay, let's do it!

Chapter 1 - Optimization Techniques

Optimization, also known as SEO, is important, and the steps described in this chapter are necessary to get your books ranked in the search engines. These are NOT tricks; these are proven techniques that work!

Step 1: Research Titles & Keywords – DO NOT <u>ONLY</u> USE Google AdWords Keyword Tool and the Global Monthly Searches of "low competition" long-tailed keyword terms! Don't do this, please! Use both Google and the Kindle Search Tool. Kindle readers go first to the Kindle Search Tool BEFORE they use the search engines! It's like a surgeon saying, "OOPS!" when you are on the operating table. Not Good! This is how you do it...

I use this FREE Keyword Pad, too, (Good Keywords) developed by Softnik:

http://www.softnik.com/products/

Here is an excellent tutorial on Keyword Pad:

http://www.tiawood.com/articles/tools/509-tools-using-keyword-pad-to-find-available-domains.html

Okay, let's demonstrate using my book Body Language:
http://www.amazon.com/dp/B006INI18G

Go to the Amazon Kindle Store:

http://www.amazon.com/kindle-store-ebooks-newspapers-blogs/b/ref=touch_wel_em_kinstore?ie=UTF8&node=133141011

In the search box enter the term - body language. You will see this:

Notice the drop down menu. These are the keywords that Kindle readers are using to find books on Body Language. Amazon Kindle Direct Publishing allows 7-

keywords so you can select keywords from the drop down menu (place in a text file)! Next, look for the bestselling book in your category – in this case. Body Language. In the above example, the book called "What every BODY is saying" is the top selling book on Body Language.

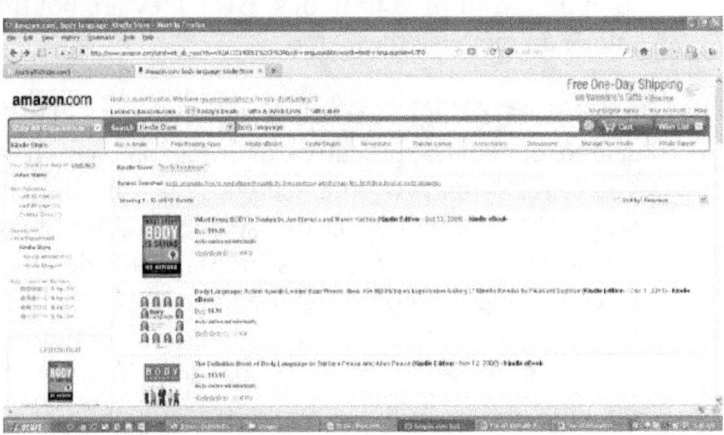

Click on the title and go to its listing. Slide down the page past the Reviews to where it says "Tags Customers Associate with This Product".

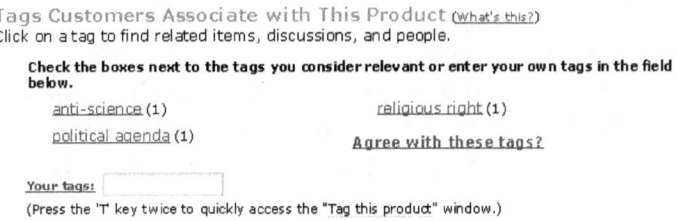

These are "customer added" tags that show the keywords that customers used to find this book on Body Language.

IMPORTANT: You can add tags to your own book, and I highly suggest you do. Just enter them in the box where it says, Your tags:

Also, Kindle Store is THE MAIN search engine you use to optimize all of your books, BUT they are not the only one. You may use these, too:

eReaderIQ: http://www.ereaderiq.com/ - This is a search engine specifically for Amazon.com. It allows you to really narrow your searches on Amazon...often in ways the normal Amazon search engine does not. eReaderIQ allows you to search the Kindle Store by price, average customer review, and publication date. It also allows you to eliminate public domain titles from a search or to search only public domain titles. Not to mention it gives you the ability to search for ebooks with those criteria...and then dig down deeper by narrowing the search by category. So if you want to find every ebook priced between $1 and $10 in the category of "Computers and Internet – Graphic Design"....you can easily accomplish that with eReaderIQ.

Jungle Search: http://www.jungle-search.com/US/ - Jungle Search is best used for searching physical/print books on Amazon. Why search for print books if our goal is to publish ebooks for the Kindle? The reason is very simple. Even with the recent "revolution" that we are seeing with ebooks, there are lots of publishers who have been slow to adjust. This means there are many print books that sell very well that are not available in ebook form.

NovelRank: http://www.novelrank.com/ - NovelRank allows you to track how many sales a book or ebook has made. All you have to do is enter the URL of the book into NovelRank, and it will track the book for you. Unfortunately, it won't tell you how many sales a book has made before that – unless it's already been entered previously into NovelRank's system. While NovelRank is not a perfect indicator of exact sales numbers, it does give you an idea of what is selling on Amazon and in the Kindle Store.

- **Pick Winning Titles** – Remember: content, book cover, and title are the most important aspects to selling ebooks online in any format, whether PDF or EPUB! Be creative and use what I call "title boosters" such as "how to, tips to, best way to, easiest way to, fastest way to, cheapest way to," etc.

- **Step 2: Create Content - Freelance it** – Write it yourself or use any of the myriad of freelance services such as Elance.com, Guru.com, or Freelancer.com.

- **Step 3: Set Up Publisher Accounts** – A list is in Chapter 7.

- **Create an Amazon Kindle account from which to sell** - https://kdp.amazon.com/self-publishing/signin. Once you have signed up, click on Add Title: Do not put in a pub date. If you have an ISBN then add it, but it is not required. Never publish private label rights material. No duplicate content is allowed and can even get your account shutdown. Amazon uses Copyscape on every

11

book   that   each   author   publishes:
http://www.copyscape.com/.

- **Here are the important inputs or "fields" that will make or break your sales and most of these are Keyword searchable**: Title, Series Title, Description, Contributors, Categories, and Keywords. I call this Direct KOP or Direct Kindle Optimization Protocol because all of it takes place within the KDP platform. Later, I will discuss Indirect KOP…

- **Book Cover** –Must be in jpeg or tiff format and 400 x 577 in size.

- **Description** – Very important since this is what shows up in the search engines. Please check the spelling and grammar before posting the description!

- **Formats -** HTML and word doc format to EPUB or XML format. I publish from my Word doc to EPUB then upload it to Kindle, and Kindle changes it to their format.

- **Best price points -** $2.99 - $9.99 price point (I prefer $8.87, $6.87, and $4.87).

- **Minimum pages -** 20-40 pages.

Paid Promotion Sites – I use these sites quite often and a couple of them can be pricey but well worth it:

http://www.pixelofink.com/
http://kindlenationdaily.com/

http://thefrugalereader.com/
http://ereadernewstoday.com/

Free Promotion Sites– Squidoo rocks and if you are not using it then you are missing out on some neat traffic and sales.

http://www.squidoo.com/the-best-of-amazon-daily-free-ebooks-kindle-ipad
http://digitalbooktoday.com/

And let's not forget Amazon's Shelfari: http://www.shelfari.com/. Shelfari is owned by Amazon and is free so take advantage of it.

Chapter 2 - Promotional Techniques

This is the important part and my favorite because I like experimenting with what works and what doesn't work!

1. First, you don't need a website to sell Kindle or any ebook but on some of my popular ebooks I do post a Wordpress blog and I have a main book site:

   http://epubwealth.com

2. After posting your blog, download and use the NextGen Gallery Wordpress plugin http://wordpress.org/extend/plugins/nextgen-gallery/to put up a gallery of your books on your Wordpress website. NextGen allows you to post a montage of your book covers and then you can place the links below. NOTE: If your books are in the KDP Select program, do not list your books; otherwise, Amazon will notify you that

you are in violation of KDP Select Terms of Use. You are allowed to post paperback and PDF versions but not digital alternatives, even your Kindle links!

- Next, get your books listed in the search engines. Too many authors think that the best way to get backlinks is to go to Fiverr.com and order backlinks. Please don't do this! My experience with Fiverr backlinks is very poor. Use this site: www.profilelinkservices.com. It costs $20 for 250 backlinks but is well worth it! Once you receive this report from Profile Link Services, copy all of the URLs in the heading "Profile Links" and go to One Hour Backlinks http://www.onehourbacklinks.comand order backlinks using all of the URLs from Profile Link Services. Add in the seven tags/keywords for the book that you used in the Kindle Direct Publishing platform when you published your book. This costs $5 for 250 backlinks. Next, once you receive the One Hour Backlinks report, copy all of the URLs in Column A and go to http://pingfarm.com and enter them in the box, add an RSS feed and one keyword and mass ping all of the URLs. You will see a significant difference in sales. Do this for each and every book you publish.

3. Make a YouTube Video Book Trailer - Do a simple PowerPoint Presentation of your book or use one of the Fiverr.com contractors below:

Promo Videos

http://fiverr.com/svippshow/make-melodic-and-captivating-promotional-video-of-your-business-website-or-product

http://fiverr.com/mmarket/create-a-professional-looking-design-video-in-full-hd-with-fast-delivery

http://fiverr.com/mmarket/make-this-professional-looking-hd-video-with-your-text-and-images-in-24-hours-or-less

Once you have your video uploaded to YouTube, remix it using various keywords so that your video shows up viral on the net under all of your 7-tags/keywords for the book that you used in the Kindle Direct Publishing platform when you published your book. Here is a sample of one of my book trailers for my novel "Common Ground":

http://youtu.be/T2bWz54k0nI

Use high competition keywords for this and not low ones. If you don't know how to remix a YouTube video then write to me mailto:lee.benton@epubwealth.com and I will bring you up on http://wwwJoin.me and by sharing my screen show you exactly how to do it.

I will go over more in my online webinars I put on for my customers. You will be notified by email. Be sure to add your name to my email list at the "ePublish Your Ebook Group":

http://forms.aweber.com/form/41/1188862441.htm

4. Order Reviews, Likes, Tags, and Sharing on social media networks such as Facebook and Twitter. I use the following two sites exclusively for everything from reviewing my videos to reviewing my books. They rock, and they are not very expensive!

https://microworkers.com
https://www.taskrabbit.com/

For example, I used Microworkers to promote my book trailer on YouTube for my novel "The Writing of the Wrong" http://youtu.be/2oV5zCQEhr4. I hired 30-microworkers, and they liked and posted favorable reviews. Last time I checked, there were 57 views so the buzz they caused got me 27 more views. When I went to check my Kindle sales for this book, I sold an additional 7-Kindle books and 5-PDFs. The Microworkers campaign cost me $11.39. Taskrabbit is like Fiverr.com. They charge $5.00 per task.

5. Check your competition to see how many reviews and backlinks they have and get more for your books to knock them out of their position:

http://www.opensiteexplorer.org/
http://ahrefs.com/

Kindle Indirect Optimization Protocol

I wanted to make this a separate section since it is really important. Indirect KOP is 3-times more important than Direct KOP described above. Here are the components to Indirect KOP:

- In researching niches, look for niches with less than 200,000 in competition.
- Use the Series Title on the KDP Publishing platform to pack in rich relevant keywords that are tied to title.

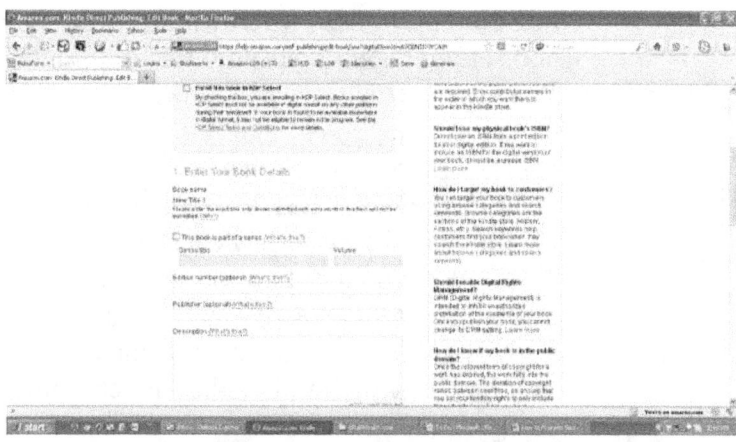

- Under Product details in the book listings, specifically under "Amazon Best Sellers Rank," check the Kindle Store listing of keywords that ranks the highest book sellers in your niche.

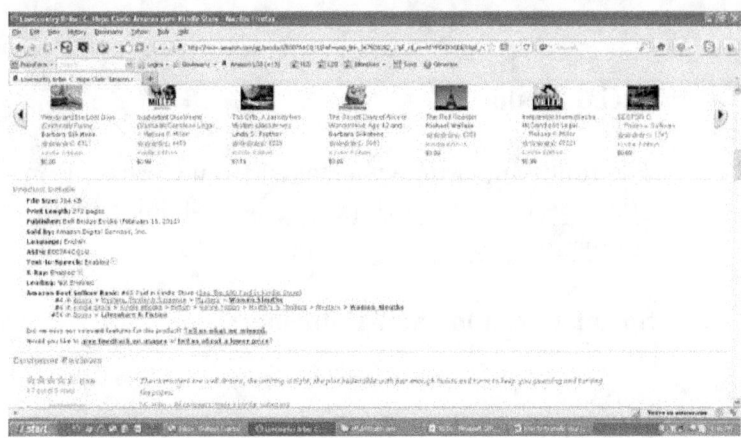

- In the left hand column of the same aforementioned book listing, specifically under "Department" notice the hidden keywords listed at the bottom.

- You can also get keyword ideas under the Tags section of the Product Description.

Social Media

The following article was taken from Gorham Printing:
http://www.gorhamprinting.com/diy-book-printing/book-publishing-social-media.html

Social Media for Self-Publishers

Large publishing houses have many resources they can utilize to market a book through national book store  chains, large magazines, and even television ads. As a self-published author, your options may be much more limited but that doesn't mean you can't still get the word out effectively and inexpensively. The internet is one of your greatest resources as it can be used for a very low cost, and often for free, to help you market your book, connect with other authors, and communicate with your fans and potential readers.

Despite the title for this section, social media should not be treated as a form of advertising. When you advertise, you have one specific goal: showcase your product in an appealing way in an attempt to get people to buy it. Ask anyone and most people will tell you they dislike advertising. So what should you use social media for? You should use it for building relationships with your readers, showcasing your knowledge, and engaging your audience.

Social media marketing takes TIME. It can take months before you feel like you're getting anywhere with it. Don't give up! Everyone who starts a new blog or Facebook page goes through the same thing. Stick with it, and you WILL reap the benefits!

Before you start, analyze these questions:

- What are my goals?
- Where is my target audience? Are they active on Facebook? Twitter? A niche site that I can participate in?
- How much time can I devote to social media?

Below are three of the most useful sites to get started with. Each one requires a slightly different strategy but used together can create a powerful network. From the following information, you can choose to do parts of it or all of it, according to the amount of time you can devote to social media and your needs.

Blogging

A blog is one of your most powerful resources as a self-publisher. If you ignore all the other marketing suggestions on this site, I strongly suggest you don't ignore this one. A blog can be one of your most effective tools.

When you begin blogging, a good place to start is to figure out a goal. As a self-published author, your goal may be to gain more visibility for your book, to become recognized as an expert in your field, or to get your name out there as an author. Figuring out your goals will give you a direction for your blog and help keep you motivated to continue blogging.

One major benefit to having a blog is that customers can find you even if they don't know who you are or that you wrote a book! For instance, if you've authored a cookbook, you might post a few of your recipes to your blog. Someone who Google's "red velvet brownie recipe" could end up on your blog and then you have a potential new reader! Blogs are also great ways to connect with current readers, other self-published authors, and potential readers.

No matter what the subject of your book, with a little creativity you can create a relevant and engaging blog. Say you've written a diet and exercise book. A blog is a great way to illustrate to your customers that what you've written about works. Share your journey to becoming a fit person. Post healthy recipes, workouts, interviews with people who have completed your program or who have successfully changed their lives, your thoughts on current weight loss trends, or anything else you can think of. A blog allows you to create trust and credibility between you and your reader, and they will be more likely to buy a book from you as they know they will be getting quality content. Even if you're not writing non-fiction, a blog can still be one of your most important assets. You can start a blog to help others on their self-publishing journey, a personal blog chronicling your life experiences or interests, a self-help blog, or a cooking blog. The content of your blog doesn't necessarily need to correlate to the books you're writing; you could focus on selling yourself. The point is to help the reader feel connected to who you are as a person and want to help support you in your endeavors.

Tips for using blogs to market your book:

- o Buy a domain name. Make sure the domain name is easy to remember and easy to spell. You can set up your blog through a free site such as wordpress.com or blogger.com. Both sites make it very simple to buy a domain name and host your site for you.
- o Update your blog often, at least 2-3 times a week. If you aren't updating with regular content, you risk losing readers who may forget about you or decide to get their content elsewhere. Create a schedule that works for you and stick to it, no matter what.

- o Make sure you have an RSS feed. Many people who read blogs organize them in a feed so that they can see many different blogs at once and are able to read your posts as soon as you hit publish. For maximum visibility, make sure your RSS feed is functional.
- o Make sure you have a readable blog design. Wordpress and Blogger both have some beautiful templates that are free to use. As a rule, dark or black text on a white or light colored background is easier to read than white text on a dark background.
- o Link to other blogs and websites. The authors of those blogs will be thankful for the recognition and may just return the favor!
- o Develop unique columns that you post weekly. Not only will this always give you something to blog about, but it could become something you are known for in the blogging world!
- o Be sure to leave comments on other blogs whose content you find useful or relevant.
- o Guest post on blogs and ask relevant bloggers to guest post on yours. This helps make their readers aware of you and vice versa.

Facebook

With millions of users and growing, Facebook is a great way to connect with potential readers and help spread the word about your book.

The first step is to set up a Fan Page. It's important to separate your personal Facebook page from your fan page. People who "like" your page are expecting to see some content relating to your book and by liking your page, they are essentially saying they're ok with that. That doesn't mean you should spam people who like your page with links to buy your book. That's a quick way to get someone to unlike your page. Always keep in mind that social media is about creating relationships with people who have similar interests as you. Be sure to like other pages that are relevant to your topic and participate in those with thoughtful discussion as well.

Getting people to like your page requires some creativity. You can offer an incentive such as a free copy of your eBook for liking your page, suggest your page to friends, promote your page in more traditional ways (put a link on business cards and other promotional material), and cross promote your Facebook page with your twitter page and blog.

There are many ways to get people engaged, so long as you're friendly, offer excellent and relevant content, and use a bit of time and effort.

Tips for marketing your book with Facebook:

- o Buy a domain name. Make sure the domain name is easy to remember and easy to spell. You can set up your blog through a free site such as wordpress.com or blogger.com. Both sites make it very simple to buy a domain name and host your site for you.
- o Don't use your personal Facebook page to bombard your friends with messages about your

books. Every couple of weeks you can update your status and remind people to "like" the fan page you set up, then through your fan page you can talk more about your book.

o Share things that you find funny or useful. Do keep in mind this is a business page so make sure anything you post is relevant to your business and tasteful.

o Try not to make selling your book the main focus of your Facebook page. Use the 80/20 rule: 80% of the content you post should be useful to the people who "liked" your page, while the other 20% can be used to promote yourself and/or your book. Figure out why your readers are following you and what information can be most useful to them and post about it.

o You need to give people a reason to "like" you on Facebook. Run a promotion. Give away digital copies of your book to each person that signs up. Be creative! You can also pay Facebook to promote your page to people with similar interests.

o Respond to your fans. Once you have the content set up and your fans start liking the page and writing responses to the things you post, be sure to write back! Let them know you're paying attention and that you appreciate their input.

o Be sure to get your own Facebook URL that you can use on any printed materials you may have. Facebook allows you to customize your URL so you can direct people to Facebook.com/YourBook.

Twitter

Twitter is an important tool for connecting with your audience and getting your name out there. Would you knock on your neighbor's door and ask him to buy your book? Of course you wouldn't! But it might come up in natural conversation that you've written a book and are selling it. If you're on good terms with your neighbor, he might be inclined to check it out.

Twitter is no different. People use twitter to connect with interesting people and talk about their day. Think of all the users on twitter as new neighbors that you haven't yet met. Your goal is to meet them, get to know them, and let them get to know you. Twitter should be used more as a way of getting your name out there. That's not to say that you can never ever mention your book. You just need to be creative about it. Give people a reason to check it out.

Be sure to spend some time building your content before you begin following other Twitter users. To other users, it can look bad when you are following a large number of people but have few followers. If you spend some time adding relevant and interesting content, some of those people you follow will gladly follow you as well!

Tips for using Twitter to market your book:

- o Search for trending topics that are relevant to your book and utilize them.
- o Communicate with your followers. Twitter is all about conversation. Use it to get closer to your readers.

- Twitter, like Facebook, is a great place to host giveaways, conduct polls, and get feedback from your readers.
- Follow relevant users, both related to your book topics as well as other self-published authors.
- Be interesting! Give people a reason to follow you. If you've never used twitter, spend some time looking at what other people are saying. Take note of what catches your eye.
- Do not use your personal account. Make a separate account that you can link to your Facebook and blog.
- Offer freebies and specials through twitter. For instance, you could host a monthly giveaway for a free eBook.
- Use an eye-catching avatar that can only be associated with you. A striking photograph of yourself, your book cover art, or a photo you took is a great avatar. Make sure it's unique and then use it throughout every social media platform you use.
- As with any social media platform, do not spam. Sending constant messages with links to where to buy your book is considered spam and will hurt your reputation. Work on building relationships with people and having conversations.
- Get feedback and engage your readers. Post a chapter of your book on twitter and ask for people's thoughts. This is a much more subtle way to advertise (and a great way to find out if you need to change anything!).

- o Search twitter and answer questions or offer your opinion if it's relevant. Be helpful and friendly. Help out other self-published authors.

Other resources

Here is a great resource to using Twitter for social media marketing. I suggest you read the entire thing before you begin. It will be very worth your time:

http://www.copyblogger.com/ultimate-twitter/

Goodreads

Goodreads.com is a place where readers get together to discover and discuss books and is an excellent community in which to get involved. You can create discussions about books, create a virtual book club, and even share your own writing. You can also set up your profile with a link to your website, blog, or Facebook page. Goodreads is made up of people who are passionate about books; many users blog about books, write lengthy reviews, and love to spend time discussing books with other people.

Once you join, a good approach would be to spend some time writing well thought-out reviews on some books in the genre of books that you're hoping to sell. This will help you gain some credibility with potential readers and help you connect with people who may be interested in the book you wrote.

Goodreads is far more community-oriented than the other suggestions on this page and definitely not a place to try to push your book on people. As with all social media, the point is to get to know people, get your name out there, and make connections.

Fiverr.com has a vendor that is excellent to assist you in getting up on Goodreads. I use this vendor every week since he publishes a good many gigs on Fiverr.com. He is also excellent for assisting you in getting set up on CreateSpace:

http://fiverr.com/jawadams/add-your-book-to-goodreads

Tips for using Goodreads to market your book:

- o Some authors have been known to "friend" hundreds of people while having only their own book on their bookshelf and don't otherwise participate in the community. Users can see right through this behavior, and they don't appreciate it.
- o There are many active authors on Goodreads. Connect with them as well as your readers and help each other out.
- o Before you jump in, spend some time reading reviews and getting a feel for the community. Figure out how you can fit in to it.

Other Social Media Avenues

Everyday more and more social media sites pop up. Below are some other suggestions that you may think about incorporating. A word of warning: don't try to do them all! Figure out how much time you can devote to social media and which sites you feel are best for you and focus just on those. You might also consider searching for niche communities related to your genre (for instance, if you write about travel, there are many travel sites you can get involved in).

- 🔍 Pinterest is an online pin board where users share websites and photos. Topics range from fitness to fashion to books.
- 🔍 Tumblr is a micro-blogging service that allows you to post videos, music, photos, text, and reblog other users content.
- 🔍 Google+ is a social site similar to Facebook. This is a good site to keep an eye on as it grows.
- 🔍 LinkedIn is a popular site used for professional networking.

Other book communities:

- 🔍 aNobii
- 🔍 weRead
- 🔍 Wattpad
- 🔍 Shelfari

Bookmarking - Top 15 Most Popular Social Bookmarking Websites | December 2012

Here are the 15 Most Popular Social Bookmarking Websites as derived from our eBizMBA Rank which is a constantly updated average of each website's Alexa

Global Traffic Rank, and U.S. Traffic Rank from both Compete and Quantcast. "*#*" Denotes an estimate for sites with limited Compete or Quantcast data.

1 | Twitter
15 - eBizMBA Rank | 250,000,000 - Estimated Unique Monthly Visitors | 30 - Compete Rank | 5 - Quantcast Rank | 9 - Alexa Rank.

Most Popular Social Bookmarking Websites | Updated 12/5/2012 | eBizMBA
2 | Reddit
295 - eBizMBA Rank | 16,000,000 - Estimated Unique Monthly Visitors | 705 - Compete Rank | 64 - Quantcast Rank | 115 - Alexa Rank.
Most Popular Social Bookmarking Websites | Updated 12/5/2012 | eBizMBA

3 | Pinterest
375 - eBizMBA Rank | 15,500,000 - Estimated Unique Monthly Visitors | 205 - Compete Rank | 811 - Quantcast Rank | 109 - Alexa Rank.
Most Popular Social Bookmarking Websites | Updated 12/5/2012 | eBizMBA

4 | StumbleUpon
416 - eBizMBA Rank | 15,000,000 - Estimated Unique Monthly Visitors | 950 - Compete Rank | *150* - Quantcast Rank | 150 - Alexa Rank.
Most Popular Social Bookmarking Websites | Updated 12/5/2012 | eBizMBA

5 | BuzzFeed

562 - eBizMBA Rank | 14,500,000 - Estimated Unique Monthly Visitors | 419 - Compete Rank | 132 - Quantcast Rank | 632 - Alexa Rank.
Most Popular Social Bookmarking Websites | Updated 12/5/2012 | eBizMBA

6 | Delicious
869 - eBizMBA Rank | 5,500,000 - Estimated Unique Monthly Visitors | 1,396 - Compete Rank | *870* - Quantcast Rank | 342 - Alexa Rank.
Most Popular Social Bookmarking Websites | Updated 12/5/2012 | eBizMBA

7 | Tweetmeme
873 - eBizMBA Rank | 5,450,000 - Estimated Unique Monthly Visitors | 1,317 - Compete Rank | 877 - Quantcast Rank | 426 - Alexa Rank.
Most Popular Social Bookmarking Websites | Updated 12/5/2012 | eBizMBA

8 | digg
1,314 - eBizMBA Rank | 4,100,000 - Estimated Unique Monthly Visitors | 3,137 - Compete Rank | 430 - Quantcast Rank | 375 - Alexa Rank.
Most Popular Social Bookmarking Websites | Updated 12/5/2012 | eBizMBA

9 | FARK
1,728 - eBizMBA Rank | 1,850,000 - Estimated Unique Monthly Visitors | 2,045 - Compete Rank | 1,019 - Quantcast Rank | 2,120 - Alexa Rank.
Most Popular Social Bookmarking Websites | Updated 12/5/2012 | eBizMBA

10 | Slashdot
1,805 - eBizMBA Rank | 1,700,000 - Estimated Unique Monthly Visitors | 2,335 - Compete Rank | *1,825* - Quantcast Rank | 1,254 - Alexa Rank.
Most Popular Social Bookmarking Websites | Updated 12/5/2012 | eBizMBA

11 | Friendfeed
2,380 - eBizMBA Rank | 1,500,000 - Estimated Unique Monthly Visitors | 4,053 - Compete Rank | *2,400* - Quantcast Rank | 686 - Alexa Rank.
Most Popular Social Bookmarking Websites | Updated 12/5/2012 | eBizMBA

12 | Clipmarks
2,541 - eBizMBA Rank | 1,400,000 - Estimated Unique Monthly Visitors | *2,800* - Compete Rank | 1,679 - Quantcast Rank | 3,145 - Alexa Rank.
Most Popular Social Bookmarking Websites | Updated 12/5/2012 | eBizMBA

13 | Newsvine
2,544 - eBizMBA Rank | 1,390,000 - Estimated Unique Monthly Visitors | 2,224 - Compete Rank | 2,020 - Quantcast Rank | 3,388 - Alexa Rank.
Most Popular Social Bookmarking Websites | Updated 12/5/2012 | eBizMBA

14 | Diigo
3,078 - eBizMBA Rank | 1,200,000 - Estimated Unique Monthly Visitors | 4,765 - Compete Rank | *2,700* - Quantcast Rank | 1,769 - Alexa Rank.

Most Popular Social Bookmarking Websites | Updated 12/5/2012 | eBizMBA

15 | DZone
6,464 - eBizMBA Rank | 325,000 - Estimated Unique Monthly Visitors | 9,527 - Compete Rank | *NA* - Quantcast Rank | 3,401 - Alexa Rank.
Most Popular Social Bookmarking Websites | Updated 12/5/2012 | eBizMBA

16 | Chime.in
8,091 - eBizMBA Rank | 250,000 - Estimated Unique Monthly Visitors | 10,357 - Compete Rank | *NA* - Quantcast Rank | 5,825 - Alexa Rank.
Most Popular Social Bookmarking Websites | Updated 12/5/2012 | eBizMBA

Now you can post to the above sites individually or use one of the following bookmaking services to do it en masse:

http://socialmarker.com/
http://socialblaster.com/
http://www.socialposter.com/
http://www.onlywire.com/

And check out this free site too:
http://bookmarkingpro.com/

Chapter 3 - Good Ol' Fashion EMAIL MARKETING

Email Sending Platforms
Hypermail
http://tinyurl.com/hypermailplatform

Velocity Software Marketing
http://www.velocitymarketingsoftware.com/

Email Lists
EmailNations
http://emailnations.com
B2B or B2C $97/list - You order by county at 435-249-5600.
Unlimited B2B or B2C Lists at $497 - You order by county at 435-249-5600.

SMS Cell Phone Numbers same as above – per list by area code ($97) or unlimited by area code ($497).

File Sharing
FileFactory
http://tinyurl.com/7ynayvn

Autoresponder
AWeber
http://bit.ly/NMxDo

CAN SPAM LAWS
http://business.ftc.gov/documents/bus61-can-spam-act-compliance-guide-business/

I use Hypermail http://tinyurl.com/hypermailplatform as my sending platform. They are good and very easy to use.

If you are going to be doing a good deal of emailing as a do-it-yourselfer, then I suggest using Hypermail because in the long run they are actually cheaper than most bulk email senders.

I have listed the Hypermail pricing below but remember these prices do not include the domain name and server.

Add an extra $30/server for the domain name and server!

Example: If you purchase the Premier package with 5-servers/3.5 million maximum emails per month @ $249, you must add 5 servers x $30 = $150 to the $249 for a total monthly cost of $399.

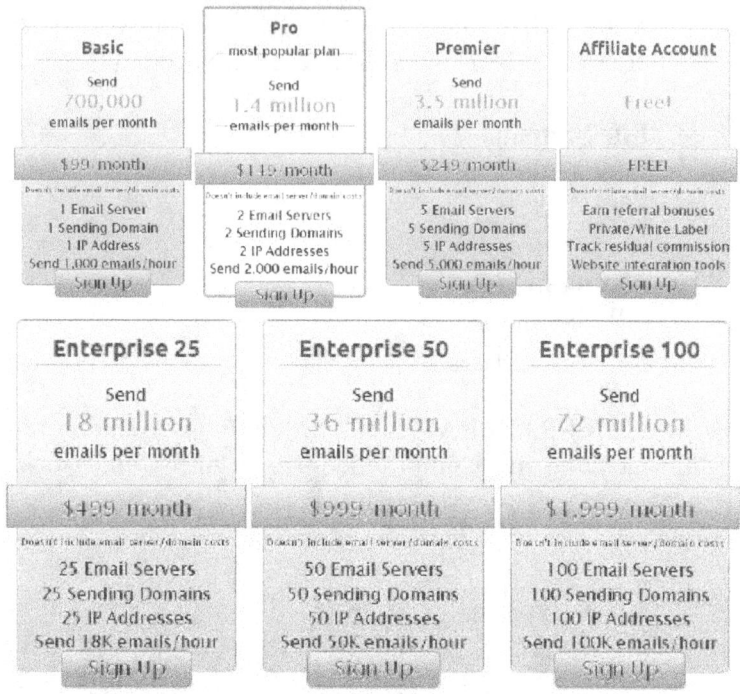

Basic	Pro most popular plan	Premier	Affiliate Account
Send 700,000 emails per month	Send 1.4 million emails per month	Send 3.5 million emails per month	Free!
$99/month	$119/month	$249/month	FREE!
Doesn't include email server/domain costs	Doesn't include email server/domain costs	Doesn't include email server/domain costs	Doesn't include email server/domain costs
1 Email Server 1 Sending Domain 1 IP Address Send 1,000 emails/hour	2 Email Servers 2 Sending Domains 2 IP Addresses Send 2,000 emails/hour	5 Email Servers 5 Sending Domains 5 IP Addresses Send 5,000 emails/hour	Earn referral bonuses Private/White Label Track residual commission Website integration tools
Sign Up	Sign Up	Sign Up	Sign Up

Enterprise 25	Enterprise 50	Enterprise 100
Send 18 million emails per month	Send 36 million emails per month	Send 72 million emails per month
$499/month	$999/month	$1,999/month
Doesn't include email server/domain costs	Doesn't include email server/domain costs	Doesn't include email server/domain costs
25 Email Servers 25 Sending Domains 25 IP Addresses Send 18K emails/hour	50 Email Servers 50 Sending Domains 50 IP Addresses Send 50K emails/hour	100 Email Servers 100 Sending Domains 100 IP Addresses Send 100K emails/hour
Sign Up	Sign Up	Sign Up

Hypermail is an unusual company insofar as they provide the sending software, the server, and domain all under one turnkey operation.

They also provide the metric reporting software that gives you amount of emails sent, views, click throughs, and Optouts.

This is important: Using the premier package once again as an example, you have five servers and each server can run a campaign.

Each server can comfortably do 1,000 emails per hour; any faster and the emails begin getting blocked by the ISPs.

38

That equates to 5,000 emails per hour and 120,000 per day.

Besides Hypermail, you need to provide the email list. I have given you a list provider above. Candidly, I am the king of book lover email lists, so talk to me first; I more than likely have what you are looking for and at prices that no one beats:

mailto:support@epubwealth.com.

Chapter 4 - Combination Marketing Techniques

In this section, you really need to pay close because it will blow the stops off your email campaigns. The best way to teach this subject is by example. One of the divisions of my company is called BookbuilderPLUS. Go look at the sales page here: http://bookbuilderplus.com. This is a $5,000 program. We ran this campaign on July 27, 2012. See the results below:

Campaign Information	
Campaign ID	195823
Title	BookbuilderPLUS1
Status	Completed
Last Update Time	July 27, 2012, 01:05:30 pm
Start Time	July 27, 2012, 04:02:45 am
End Time	July 27, 2012, 01:05:41 pm
List	TX_B2B_Dallas County1
Subject	Use the power of ePublishing to increase customer traffic to your business
Message	Use the power of ePublishing to increase customer traffic to Your Business.
Suppression	
Domain	whitelistproducts.net
IP Address	76.73.71.18
From Name	Leland Benton
From Address	support
Send To:	Full
Start Index	0
End Index	0
DKIM	Yes
Domain Delivery Groups	Yes
Sent	346,387
Sending Speed	Average
Views	913 (Open Log)
Clicks	6,619 (Click Log)
Optouts	86
Forwards	0
Social Shares	0 (Get Sharing Code)

We sent 346,387 emails to Dallas County, TX. There were 913 views and 6,619 clicks. The reason for the high click volume is that there were multiple hyperlinks in the email.

We then ran a similar campaign in Tarrant County, TX but combined it with a TV ad and the response was a 400% increase over just an email campaign alone.

The TV ad we used is here: http://youtu.be/oUfwolfxK1E.

The TV ad cost $495 to create (Low Cost TV Ads is in the Appendix) and I purchased $2,000 in TV spots from Television Ad Group (also in the Appendix).

41

Do not discount Combination Marketing; it works and it works well! TV stations and cable TV stations are starving for business, and ad spots are really low. Take advantage of this fact.

SMS/MMS Mobile Marketing

Another great combination marketing technique is using SMS/MMS with email marketing. This isn't a guidebook on SMS/MMS Mobile Marketing, so I won't get into detail here. My book, "Selling Air" is my bible when it comes to mobile marketing.

Suffice it to say that SMS works a good deal better than MMS because it reaches everywhere. I personally don't do very much MMS but more so because I believe it is pretty saturated. SMS, on the other hand, is wide open and like I said previously, many smaller communities go untouched and are ripe for the picking.

Amazon Publishing

As I said previously, I make a very healthy monthly income as a Kindle book author. Presently, I have over 200 books on Amazon under various pen names. I almost exclusively promote my books using email. Here's an example…

Bully America
What is happening to our children?

Dr. Leland Benton

One of my books is called "Bully America" and is about what is happening to our children today as evidenced by the bullying of the New York bus monitor Karen Kline.

Now a good many Kindle authors buy expensive programs to teach them how to promote their books. My way is easier, quicker, and sells a ton of books. Look at the results of one of my email campaigns below. I sent the book out to a general B2B list of 912,588 that covered the continental USA. I received 1,088 views and 288 clicks. And although the email software doesn't record sales, I received 138 sales from this campaign.

Campaign Information	
Campaign ID	195963
Title	Bully America
Status	Completed
Last Update Time	July 28, 2012, 09:36:25 pm
Start Time	July 27, 2012, 09:37:27 am
End Time	July 28, 2012, 09:36:42 pm
List	USA_B2B_4
Subject	Here is a special offer on the bgest-selling book "Bully America".
Message	Here is a special offer on the best-selling book "Bully America"...
Suppression	
Domain	whitelistproducts.net
IP Address	76.73.71.18
From Name	Dr. Leland Benton
From Address	support
Send To:	Full
Start Index	0
End Index	0
DKIM	Yes
Domain Delivery Groups	Yes
Sent	912,588
Sending Speed	Average
Views	1,088 (Open Log)
Clicks	288 (Click Log)
Optouts	29
Forwards	0
Social Shares	0 (Get Sharing Code)

Now, this is also important because of the low margins paid on Kindle books and because Amazon pays 60-days in the arrears, you cannot combine TV advertising with this type of promotion; the margins are too low. However, if you publish in paperback using Createspace or Lulu.com, there are enough margins to do a combination marketing campaign.

Here is another example…

The Power of Observation is a Kindle book that now ranks 153,238 on Kindle. When it was first published, it ranked 832,144. We ran a series of campaigns one of which is displayed below. In this campaign, we sent 625,955 messages to targeted book lovers in the USA.

This was not a specific geo-targeted list but encompassed book lovers all over the USA. The campaign received 1324 views with 281 clicks to the landing page. From these 281 clicks, there were 98 sales. The campaign took all of 10-minutes to launch and the actual run time was about 12-hours. Now this is important…When a purchase is made, it takes the buyer to PayPal. Once the purchase is made, it takes the buyer to an AWeber info box and captures the buyer's info. It then automatically sends the buyer to the download link to receive the book. But the system captures the email addresses of everyone that viewed the landing page as well as everyone that clicked to the landing page. Both are captured in a CSV log that you can download, which enables you to do a follow-up mailing.

Campaign Information	
Campaign ID	195976
Title	Power of Observation
Status	Completed
Last Update Time	July 28, 2012, 09:36:14 am
Start Time	July 27, 2012, 10:09:06 am
End Time	July 28, 2012, 09:36:29 am
List	USA_B2B_3
Subject	The Power of Observation trains you to see and hear everything...
Message	The Power of Observation trains you to see and hear everything...
Suppression	
Domain	whitelistproducts.net
IP Address	76.73.71.18
From Name	Dr. Leland Benton
From Address	support
Send To:	Full
Start Index	0
End Index	0
DKIM	Yes
Domain Delivery Groups	Yes
Sent	625,995
Sending Speed	Average
Views	1,324 (Open Log)
Clicks	281 (Click Log)
Optouts	77
Forwards	0
Social Shares	0 (Get Sharing Code)

BIG Note: Although there are millions of Kindle and other eReader devices in the marketplace, the bulk of your sales will be for the PDF version of your book. In fact, statistically, the ratio is 4-PDF sales to 1-Kindle sale.

 Here is another campaign for The Power of Observation to compare. This campaign went to another USA book lover list. The total messages sent were 347,180.There were 196 opens and a total of 96 clicks to the landing page. This resulted in 21 buys. The most important aspect of this program is the targeted list, and we are constantly refining and testing these lists.

Campaign Information	
Campaign ID	196252
Title	The Power of Observation
Status	Completed
Last Update Time	July 29, 2012, 10:43:13 pm
Start Time	July 29, 2012, 09:54:44 am
End Time	July 29, 2012, 10:43:17 pm
List	USA B2B 1
Subject	The Power of Observation trains you to see and hear everything...
Message	The Power of Observation trains you to see and hear everything...
Suppression	
Domain	whitelistproducts.net
IP Address	76.73.71.18
From Name	Dr. Leland Benton
From Address	support
Send To:	Full
Start Index	0
End Index	371266
DKIM	Yes
Domain Delivery Groups	Yes
Sent	347,180
Sending Speed	Average
Views	196 (Open Log)
Clicks	96 (Click Log)
Optouts	2
Forwards	0
Social Shares	0 (Get Sharing Code)

Chapter 5 - Book Tours & Event Marketing Techniques

Without a doubt, my most favorite form of promotion is book tours. There are two kinds – virtual or online book tours and physical tours inside bookstores, conventions, etc. The following vendors are the ones I use to book all of my authors' book tours:

TLC Book Tours
http://tlcbooktours.com/
Nurture Your Books
http://nurtureyourbooks.com/
Pump Up Your Book Promotion
http://www.pumpupyourbookpromotion.com/

Prices vary from $199 to $799 so check out each site to find the best one for your needs and budget.

Go here to get an idea of what a book tour looks like:

http://unconventionalbooktour.com/

If money is tight and budget is a consideration then use these people. It costs only $50:

http://www.promotionalbooktours.com/mini-book-tour/

Also be aware that there are "boutique" book tour providers that specialize in certain genres. Here is one that specializes in paranormal books:

http://bewitchingbooktours.blogspot.com/

If you use book tours correctly, you will see a very significant jump in your sales and of course they are fun, too. My authors love them and love the sales they bring in, too.

Start out slow and test the waters to see if this type of promotion is best for you.

Now this is important. I talk to a good many authors worldwide daily. I spoke to a lady in Michigan just yesterday who has two cookbooks published on Kindle. When I asked her how her sales were going, she replied, "Good. I am selling about 4-per day on each book". Listen up cowboys and cowgirls, 4-sales/day sucks! My sister has 6-cookbooks on a dozen platforms, and her Kindle sales are about 40-books/day for each book!

But in order to get these types of sales figures requires dedicated book promotion. In the next chapter, I will be describing the platforms you should be published on. There are both DIY platforms and ePublishing ones under the Directory of ePublishers that are like my company that publish books for authors. Please don't confuse the two types.

Chapter 6 - EPublishing Platforms Your Books Need To Be On

The Most Important DIY Platforms

Amazon Kindle
https://kdp.amazon.com/self-publishing/signin

BNPubIt: The Nook
http://pubit.barnesandnoble.com/pubit_app/bn?t=pi_reg_home

Lulu: Publish to the iPad
http://www.lulu.com/publish/ebooks/?cid=us_home_nav_ebk

Smashwords: 25,000 ebooks on the shelf
http://www.smashwords.com/

Google eBooks: Do it yourself — literally
http://books.google.com/ebooks

FastPencil: ebook publishing made simple
http://www.fastpencil.com/

BookLocker: No-frills self-publishing
http://www.booklocker.com/

Diesel Ebook Store
http://diesel-ebooks.com/

Kobo Books
http://www.kobobooks.com/

Sony eReader
https://ebookstore.sony.com/

Digioh
https://digioh.com/Sell-
Ebooks?gclid=CL7N9_C27awCFcdgTAodrFQRsg

Overdrive
http://www.overdrive.com/

BookBaby
http://www.bookbaby.com/

CreateSpace
http://www.createspace.com

Fiverr.com has vendors that can assist you in getting your books up on the platforms listed above. They offer services from formatting your books to each platform's requirement to cover design and cover formatting. Use them! They are inexpensive and good but be sure to check their ratings to see if they are delivering quality work. Like just about everything in life, Fiverr.com isn't the only game in town. I use the following vendor platforms that are just like Fiverr.com:

http://fittytown.com/
http://fourerr.com/
http://gigbucks.com/
http://www.gigme5.com/
http://justafive.com/
http://tenbux.com/
http://www.zeerk.com/
http://www.writeswap.com/
http://www.twentyville.com/

How to Choose an EPublisher

If you have taken the time to write a book, then it only makes sense that you should take the time to find the

54

right publisher for your work. If you decide to ePublish your book, be sure to carefully review epublishers before making a decision. There are a variety of models of ebook publishing, each with its own advantages and disadvantages. Think ahead and make a list of questions and wants you have regarding your book. See which epublisher matches the most of your needs and gives the best answers to your questions. You should still keep traditional publishers in mind for your book or novel because many of them have or will be developing ebook imprints and releasing their existing books as electronic books. Here are some of the issues you should consider in your hunt for an epublisher:

Contracts: Read the contract very carefully. If possible, have an attorney look over the contract, especially if you have concerns. Look closely at royalties, advances (if any), costs, and rights. What rights do you retain in your work? What rights does the publisher take? How many books do you get for your own use and for use as review copies? If you need more do you get an author discount? How often do you get paid royalties?

Formatting: In what type of format must you submit your work? Can you check for errors before the final publication? What if you have changes? How do you submit cover art, author photos, and other information? What about ISBN numbers?

Pod: Is print-on-demand publishing offered? Electronic books are great, but they have not yet reached mass acceptance by the consumers or reviewers. In the meantime, POD can help you get your book to readers in a format they are familiar with. Check to see if POD is an option.

Editing: Are the books edited or proofread or are they printed "as is"? Are additional fees charged for editing or proofreading? If editing services are offered, who are the editors? What experience do they have? You might want to read some books by other authors published by the epublisher to get a feel for the quality of the editing. If the epublisher has an open submissions policy and does not provide editing, you might consider using an editing service or hiring a freelance editor to proof your work for you prior to publication. It is a rare writer indeed that needs no editing at all.

Business Model: Although Internet companies are new and exciting, many of them have poor business models. Many of these companies aren't going to make it. Be sure to carefully review the company's business model. It doesn't do you any good to publish a book through an epublisher or publishing service if that company is out of business two months later.

Promotional Benefits: Does the publisher promote its authors? Does it contact the media for you? Does it compensate you for any promotional expenses? Does it offer online chats on their website? Does it have a media contact list or a mailing list where you can announce your book? How is review copies handled? How does the publisher feature its most recent releases? Many subsidy publishers offer "publish only" deals; all marketing and promotion are your responsibility. There is nothing wrong with this approach but be sure you know what the company's policies are so that you aren't disappointed.

Book Covers: Book cover graphics are a real draw at bricks-and-mortar bookstores; the same is true on the Internet. A killer cover design can help your book stand out and increase sales, so it is important that the epublisher provides attractive covers or, if not, find out if there is a way you can submit your own cover art. You should hire an artist or graphics designer, if need be.

Blurb, Sample Chapter, and Synopsis: Who writes the book synopsis for marketing purposes? Can the publisher help you find another author to blurb your book? Does your contract allow you to use part of your work for marketing? Will the publisher display a sample chapter in their online bookstore?

Book Price: How much will your book cost? How much will readers have to pay for your book? How does it compare to the price of other books in major bookstores? Is it too expensive? If the epublisher has deals with retailers, will the price of your book differ there than it does at the ePublisher's bookstore?

Delivery Time: How long does it take for your book to be published after you have signed the contract and submitted the book? Also, how long does it take the epublisher to deliver purchased books to consumers? Are delivery times consistent?

Retail Partners: Who are the ePublisher's retail partners? Does the publisher have agreements with

Amazon.com, BN.com, and/or Borders.com? What price will readers have to pay for your book at these retailers? Is there a discount or co-op available? How long will it take your book to be delivered to customers? A slow delivery time is a real turn-off to readers. How good is their relationship with these retailers?

Online Bookstore: How does the publisher promote its books? Does it have a bookstore on its website? Is it highly visible or hard to find? Does it get much traffic? Does it have a bestseller list? Does the bookstore have secure online ordering? Does the publisher take phone orders? A great online bookstore is essential, especially if you are sending people to the website to buy your book. Some epublishers offer you a higher commission for sales through their bookstore -- but this doesn't do you any good if they are not running a highly visible bookstore with reliable online ordering and quick delivery.

Sales: Will you have access to sales information? How often is it updated? If there is an online bookstore, can you find out how many people have accessed your book's page or description?

Troubleshooting: If you have a problem or a question, is there someone available by email or phone? Is there a support area on the website? How big is the staff?

Independent Resources: Be sure to check some independent resources for information about the epublisher you are considering -- do not rely solely on the information provided by the company itself or a website or service the epublishing company owns, as they tend to be biased.

Networking: What do other writing professionals think about the company? Talk to professionals in the community, including authors, editors, and publishers and get their honest opinion to help you make an evaluation. Also get opinions from friends, newsgroups, writer's groups, and professional organizations.

*e*Publishing

Directory of ePublishers

All Romance Books – romance only
http://www.allromanceebooks.com/

Amber Quill Press - all genres
http://www.amberquill.com/

Amira Press - open to erotic romance submissions only
http://www.amirapress.com/

Atlantic Bridge Publishing - all genres
http://www.atlanticbridge.net/

Awe-Struck E-Books - currently seeking SF, romantic suspense, and paranormal romance manuscripts only [imprint of Mundania Press LLC]
http://www.awe-struck.net/

Belgrave House - women's fiction, Regency romance, mystery, romantic suspense, and young adult fiction
http://www.belgravehouse.com/

Booklocker - all genres
http://www.booklocker.com/

Champagne Books - romance, SF/F, steampunk
http://www.champagnebooks.com/

CobbleStone Press, LLC - romance
http://www.cobblestone-press.com/

Diskus Publishing - all genres
http://www.diskuspublishing.com/

DLSIJ Press - publishers and distributors of electronic books for the women's community
http://dlsijpress.com/

Double Dragon Publishing - all genres
http://www.double-dragon-ebooks.com/

Dragonfly Publishing Inc.
http://www.dragonflypubs.com/

eBooksonthe.net - all genres. [Imprint of Write Words, Inc.]
http://www.ebooksonthe.net/

Echelon Press - all genres
http://www.echelonpress.com/

Ellora's Cave Publishing - romantica(tm)
http://www.ellorascave.com/

Fictionwise - all genres
http://www.fictionwise.com/servlet/mw?a=jump&id=214
18&u=/home.html

Hardshell Word Factory - all genres. [Imprint of
Mundania Press LLC]
http://www.hardshell.com/

LionHearted Publishing ® - romance
http://www.lionhearted.com/

Liquid Silver Books - SF/F and romance. [Imprint of
Atlantic Bridge]
http://www.liquidsilverbooks.com/

Literary Road - all genres
http://www.literaryroad.com/

Loose Id (tm) - cross-genre romance
http://www.loose-id.com/

Mundania Press LLC - historical, horror, mystery, SF/F,
and Romance
http://www.mundania.com/

New Concepts Publishing - all genres
http://www.newconceptspublishing.com/

Paladin Timeless Books - cross-genre, specialty/New
Age, and literary

Scorpius Digital Publishing - SF/F and horror
http://www.paladintimelessbooks.com/

Speculation Press - science fiction, fantasy, and alternate history
http://speculationpress.com/

Swimming Kangaroo - all genres
http://www.swimmingkangaroo.com/

SynergEbooks - all genres
http://www.synergebooks.com/

The Fiction Works - audio books and ebooks in all genres
http://www.fictionworks.com/

The Wild Rose Press – romance
http://www.thewildrosepress.com/

Twilight Times Books - cross-genre, specialty/New Age, and literary
http://www.twilighttimesbooks.com/

Uncial Press - fantasy, historical romance, mystery, and paranormal
http://www.uncialpress.com/

Vinspire Publishing - historical, mystery, paranormal, etc. [formerly Vintage Romance]
http://www.vrpublishing.com/index.php

Whiskey Creek Press - all genres

http://www.whiskeycreekpress.com/

Wings ePress Inc. - all genres
http://www.wings-press.com/

Writers Exchange E-Publishing - all genres
http://www.writers-exchange.com/

Zumaya Publications LLC - all genres
http://www.zumayapublications.com/

Additional ePublishers
These publishers have not been evaluated. They may
or may not offer their services for a fee.

Action Tales.com
ActionTales.com has merged with ForemostPress.com
http://www.actiontales.com/

Alexandria Digital Literature
 In the process of reorganizing
http://www.alexlit.com/

Changling Press - erotica novellas
http://www.changelingpress.com/

CityScape Books
http://cityscapebooks.co.uk/

ClockTower Books - fiction and non-fiction
**now an imprint of Infonana.com*
http://www.infonana.com/ctb/

Crowsnest EBook Publishing - SF, fantasy, horror
http://www.computercrowsnest.com/greennebula/bkindex.htm

Delphi Books
http://www.theauthorsstudio.org/delphi/

eBooks UK
http://www.ebooks-uk.com/

Electron Press - publishes quality fiction and non-fiction. Not interested in romance, fantasy, science fiction, or new age books

FairGo E-Books
http://www.electronpress.com/

GLB Publishers (R) - "literate erotica" and non-erotic works
http://www.glbpubs.com/

Inara Press – romance
http://www.inarapress.com/

Jacobyte Books - all genres
http://www.jacobytebooks.com/

Livewire Publishing - romance fiction
http://www.livewirepublishing.com.au/

London Circle Publishing - mystery, romance, non-fiction

http://www.londoncircle.com/index.shtml

MountainView Publishing -   [imprint of Treble Heart Books]
Submissions by invitation only
http://www.trebleheartbooks.com/MVWelcome.html

SANDS Publishing LLC - all genres
http://www.sandspublishing.com/

Scheherazade Tales Romance E-Novels - novel must be a tale of romance
http://scheherazadetales.com/

Silver Lake Publishing - all genres
http://www.silverlakepublishing.com/

Tyrannosaurus Press - seeking SF and fantasy works
http://www.tyrannosauruspress.com/

Additional Resources

Eguild - an organization of e-published authors. Mission statement: To promote electronic publishing and defend the rights of electronically published authors
http://www.yahoogroups.com/subscribe/Eguild

EPIC - Electronically Published Internet Connection
http://www.epicauthors.com/

Internet Publishing - fantasy author Piers Anthony lists dozens of epublishers as well as POD publishers http://www.hipiers.com/publishing.html

KnowBetter.com - listings for over 200 publishers, 120+ ebookstores, discussion boards and more. Terrific resource
http://www.knowbetter.com/

Mary Wolf's Guide to Electronic Publishers
http://www.maryzwolf.com/epub.html

Spilled Candy – promotions
http://www.spilledcandy.com/

TeleRead - Bring the E-books Home
http://www.teleread.org/

Twilight Times Books - literary, SF/F, and New Age books
http://www.twilighttimesbooks.com/
Check out the freebies page and the small press publisher's resource page

Writing-World.com - articles on epublishing and publisher links
http://www.writing-world.com/

Chapter 7 - Audio Books

Audio books rock! And they can be very lucrative. You can record them yourself or contract them out. I have done it both ways. If you do it yourself, this is important:

Set your recording to:
Constant bitrate
44.1 KHz
16-bit
2-channel stereo files
320Bps
Lame dll file

MP2 Album Requirements:
Cover jpeg 1448 x 1448 pixels
Not include audio CD logo
Not be a product shot of a CD or cassette tape

Here are some resources below:

Free Recording Software
http://audacity.sourceforge.net/

AUDIOBOOK CREATION EXCHANGE

http://www.acx.com/help/what-s-the-deal/200497690

CuePrompter.com
http://cueprompter.com/

If you are not familiar with audio books, go here and download one for free:

http://www.openculture.com/freeaudiobooks

This site has over 450 free audio books to choose from (see the listing).

There are numerous audio book platforms on which you can publish your audio books; the biggest being Amazon's Audible.com.

http://www.audible.com/
http://www.amazon.com/b?ie=UTF8&node=2402172011
https://itunes.apple.com/us/genre/audiobooks/id50000024
http://www.barnesandnoble.com/u/Audio-Books-CD-MP3-Audiobooks/379003297/
http://audioforbooks.com/buy-digital-audio-books/
http://www.booksfree.com/
http://librivox.org/
http://help.overdrive.com/audiobooks

The Amazon-owned digital audiobooks site Audible.com is launching a new program, "Audible Author Services," that pays audiobook authors $1 per sale through Audible.com, Audible.co.uk, and iTunes out of a $20 million fund. The audiobook publishers do not receive any of the funds.

To sign up, authors must make their titles available as audiobooks through Audible.com. (Audible encourages them to do this via ACX, the audiobook rights marketplace it launched last year.) Once they enroll their books in the program, Audible says, they will:

- Receive an honorarium of $1 per unit sold at Audible.com, Audible.co.uk, and iTunes, and increase awareness of their book in audio format; [**LHO note:** Downloads via subscriptions count as sales]
- Obtain samples and links from Audible for use in social media, blogs, or on their websites – wherever they communicate most easily with their fans – as part of our "quick start" audio awareness plan;

- Gain direct interaction with Audible marketing and merchandising teams; and
- Obtain a free copy of their audiobook from Audible.

Authors get an "honorarium," publishers get nothing! Significantly, the audiobooks' publishers are cut out of the deal — the $1 per unit payment is an "honorarium," "a direct payment from us to you, a way for us to reward you for promoting your work. Sharing the payment with your agent is at your discretion." Audible continues to pay regular royalties on each audiobook sold.

While Audible encourages authors to market their audiobooks, they can get the $1/sale payment without doing any extra marketing at all. The authors get $1 whether the audiobook is sold outright or downloaded as part of a monthly or annual subscription.

Chapter 8 - Automated Postcards

http://www.expresscopy.com/

Income Disclaimer: Every effort has been made to accurately represent our product and its potential. Any claims made of actual earnings or examples of actual results can be verified upon request. The testimonials and examples used are exceptional results and don't apply to the average purchaser and are not intended to represent or guarantee that anyone will achieve the same or similar results. Each individual's success depends on his or her background, dedication, desire, and motivation. As with any business endeavor, there is an inherent risk of loss of capital, and there is no guarantee that you will earn any money.

The Postcarders Direct Mail Program

1. Getting Started Fast – Doing it the right way all of the time…

First of all, I want you to learn this program the correct way and not learn any bad habits. This is a business…a real J.O.B. so diligence and application of the principles I will be teaching you are paramount in order to become successful. Please do not cut any corners! This course is laid out in the exact sequence you need to evaluate and begin ALL postcard mailing campaigns. It is comprehensive and concise with a good amount of material being discussed and covered; however, every aspect presented in this guidebook needs to be learned and committed to memory. I have included the following outline:

1. Getting Started Fast – Doing it the right way all of the time...

2. The Marketplace...

3. Product Evaluation & Determination...

4. The Fundamentals of the Mailing List...

5. The Design, Layout, and Printing of the Postcard...

6. The Recorded Sales Message...

7. The Operator Closing Call...

8. Testing Your Campaign...

9. Understanding the Costs...

10. Completely Automate the Whole Program...

Remember: there are two types of postcard marketing programs being marketed online today, and both forms are successful if conducted properly, but one is more profitable than the other. Then there are two other programs that only I offer. Here are all four of the programs:

1. ☑ **The Replicated Program** - The first is called a **"replicated program"** where you mail out postcards getting people to buy the exact same program you purchased. Most of them cost about $98 - $249 and they send you an instruction manual showing you how to work the program, where to buy postcards (printing), postage, mailing lists, etc., and direct your new customers to your replicated website.

2. ☑ **The Products Program** - Then there is the "products program" that shows you how to market real PRODUCTS that have various net profit margins, and this is where you can make some very serious coin.

3. ☑ **The Automated Program** - Once you begin making money, I will show you how to completely automate the whole process from A to Z. Everything described above in the "replicated program" and the "products program" is done automatically! The only things you do are research, find the product, and participate in the design of the postcard.

The following guidebook is everything you need to know in order to implement all three programs:

Let's begin…

The very best products to market using postcard marketing are info products. First off, there is no inventory and the shipping and handling charge most often covers all overhead (more on this later).

When I sell products using postcard marketing, I am looking for a price point (the sales price) to be 10-30 times the mark-up of my cost. For example, if I buy an info product for $7, I would then expect to sell it for $70-$210.

With these facts in mind I know what you're thinking, "I can handle that so how do I do it?" First I want you to keep one keyword in mind - "Targeting" and with this one keyword in mind let's begin with "FINANCIAL TARGETING".

Determine Your Own Paycheck (Financial Target)

REMEMBER I SAID THAT YOU CAN ACTUALLY DETERMINE YOUR OWN PAYCHECK? Did you think I was kidding you? Ha, ha! I wasn't; you will quickly learn that postcard marketing is nothing but a "numbers" game. Let me show you what I mean and hold on to your hats because this is exciting…

Let's say, for example, that you mail out 1000 postcards for a $59 info product (in actuality you will be doing this a lot because you must always test a product first and the minimal test is 1000 postcards).

Assume your response rate of 1% is decent, 1.5% is good, and 2% is great.

Your best price point is always between $59 and $99.00 but in this case we will call it $59.

Finally, let's say you want to make $150,000 in order to buy a piece of real estate.

Note: I am not saying $150,000/year but specifically $150,000 before taxes selling a $59 product with a 1% response rate and S&H covers the CTO (CTO mean cash to overhead, which means the S&H charge covers your overhead).

Let's do the math…

1000 postcards x 1% response rate = 10 sales x $59 sale price of product = $590 Gross revenue

$590 - $400 (average postage/1000) = $190 Net revenue

Note: For demo purposes, I am not including printing (this is minimal, and I will show you how to do this CHEAP), and the cost for the list because a 1% response rate is rarely achieved (usually 2-6% is more like it).

$150,000 / $190 = 789 (you will need to mail 789,000 postcards to make $150,000)

Pretty simple, eh? Now you know what is REQUIRED to make a set amount of money.

The speed of mailing and amount of postcards you mail are always in your control.

YOU SET YOUR OWN PAYCHECK!

There Are Eight Steps to Creating a Successful Postcard Campaign

1. Pick a market
2. Pick a product
3. Pick a mailing list
4. Create a postcard
5. Write a recorded sales message or Press 1 script
6. Write closing script for operator that takes order
7. Test project
8. Mail it

Here is the sequence of events from beginning to end:

◉ Mail postcard

◉ Customer calls toll free number on card

◉ Customer listens to your recorded message that explains and sells the product (usually message length is 1.5 minutes - 6 minutes)

◉ Customer is convinced and pushes 1

◉ Live operator takes order

◉ Product is shipped

NOTE: The postcard DOES NOT sell anything; and never sell a product that the customer has to go online to download...NEVER! This is a direct mail business. You mail the product out or it is done for you by a fulfillment house (more on this later in the course).

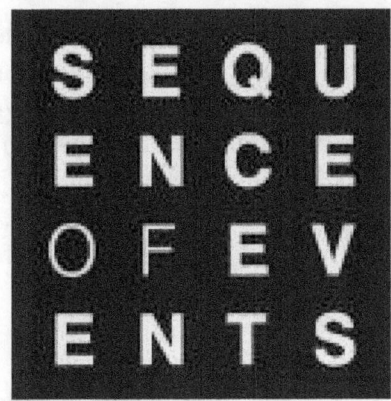

2. The Marketplace…

You are looking for **target** markets!!!!!

There are two kinds of target markets; we call them "niche" markets and "mass" markets.

Here are some things to know about both:

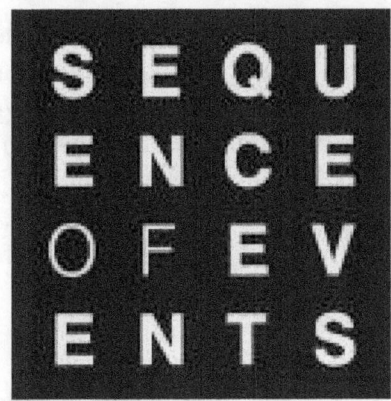 Niche markets like foot doctors vs. mass markets like nutrition or diets.
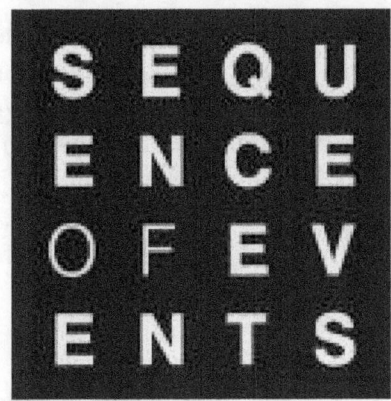 Niche markets are easier to sell to.
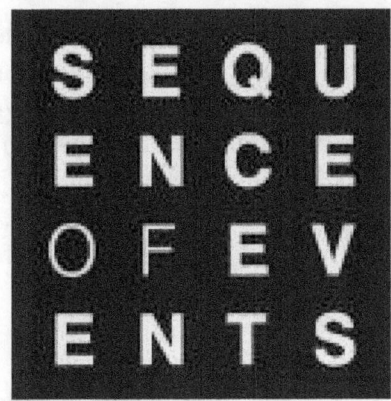 Mass market hits are more profitable.
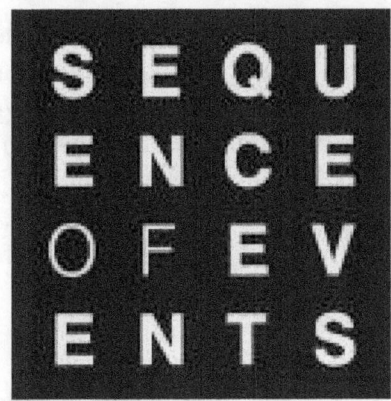 Mass markets are BEST!

*NOTE: The market you choose must have mailing lists available. Here is where I research and buy a good many of my lists: Nextmark.com: http://www.nextmark.com. This is a great company that provides listings of commercially available mailing lists and a search engine for mailing lists.

You want a market that will buy anything or everything that applies to their market for example, Harley Davidson owners, golfers, Mac computer owners.

You want an expanding market or one with new people coming in (hotline lists, more later on this term) i.e. home-based business.

Huge markets i.e. Opportunities Junkies replenishes itself weekly as do health & nutrition.

Use Google: http://www.google.com to research using lists from Nextmark and see how many people are searching online for the products these lists satisfy.

Next, use Google Insights: http://www.google.com/insights/search/ to see if the product is trending upwards or downwards.

See below...to see all of the screen shots better, increase your viewing screen to 150% using the toolbar above.

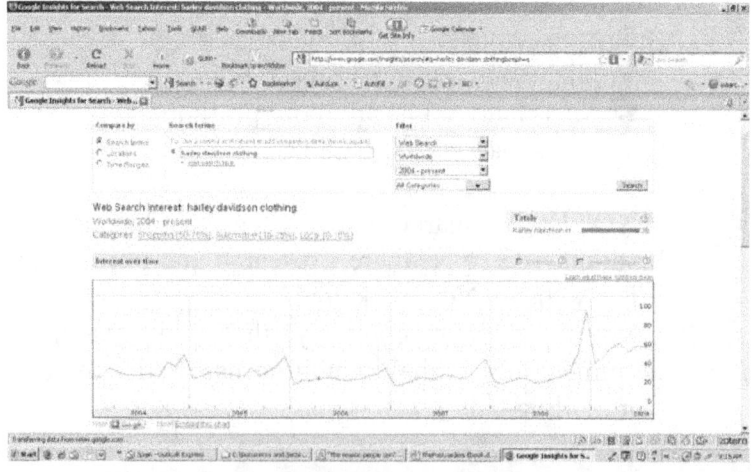

78

I wanted to know the trending patterns for "Harley Davidson Clothing". Look at the graph above. It shows that the demand dropped significantly at the end of 2008 and the beginning of 2009 but is gradually trending upwards. Looks good so far... Next Google Insights shows you where your market is:

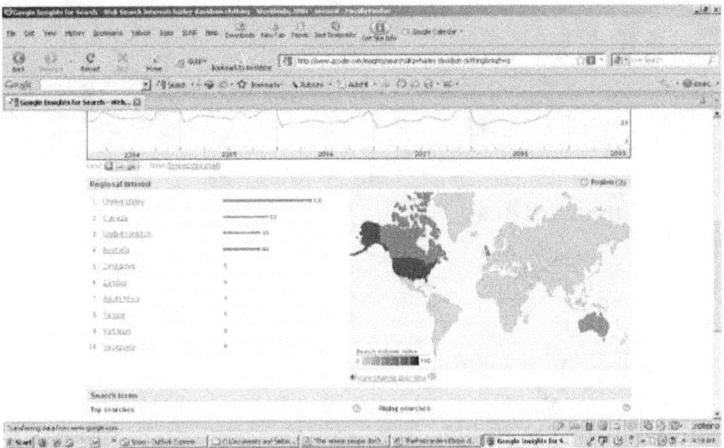

It looks like the United States, Canada, The United Kingdom, and Australia. The bulk of the market is the United States, so it is looking really good. Next, it shows you what search term received the most attention:

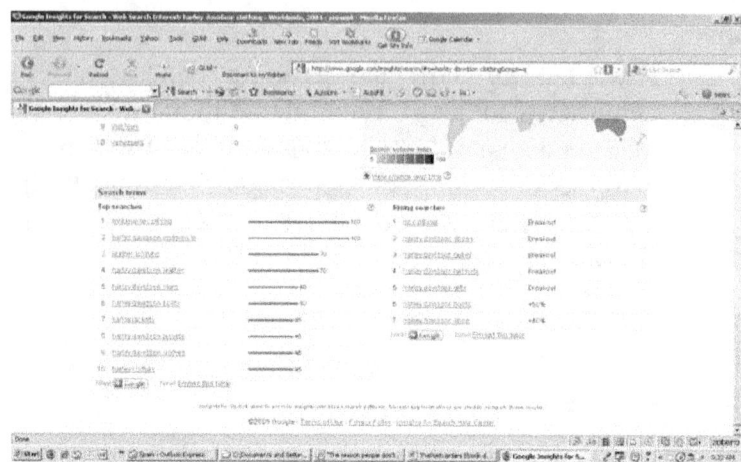

Top searches

motorcycle
clothing
harley davidson
motorcycle
leather clothing
harley   davidson
leather
harley   davidson
store
harley   davidson
boots
harley jackets
harley   davidson
jackets
harley   davidson
clothes
harley clothes

It doesn't get any easier than this, people. This is a good one to test!

Before we move on to delve more deeply into products always check and see what your competitors are doing. What are your competitors selling? Are they using a Push 1 program? Don't be surprised to find them living in the past. I don't know anybody else that conducts postcard marketing like I do.

3. Product Evaluation & Determination...

Let's talk more about identifying profitable products to sell. First understand the characteristics of profitable products:

- Strong appeal to your target market.
- Best price points $39, $59, $69, $99!
- You can break price points down into payments.
- You need really good margins 8-10 times bare minimum.
- Example: if the product cost $10 you need to sell it at $80 - $100.
- Marketing costs will eat up a minimum of 50% of your profit!
- Low shipping costs – i.e. Info products, supplements.
- Short lead time - low inventory and readily available.
- Long shelf life - info or educational product that is evergreen or never go out of date.
- Internet info products go out quickly.

Best Ways to Find Products

Look at what the people in your target market are buying by checking Nextmark. http://www.nexmark.com.

Here are the results of entering "Harley Davidson clothing" in the search box in the upper right hand corner of Nextmark's home page. **Again, to see the screen shots better, increase your viewing screen to 150% in the toolbar above.**

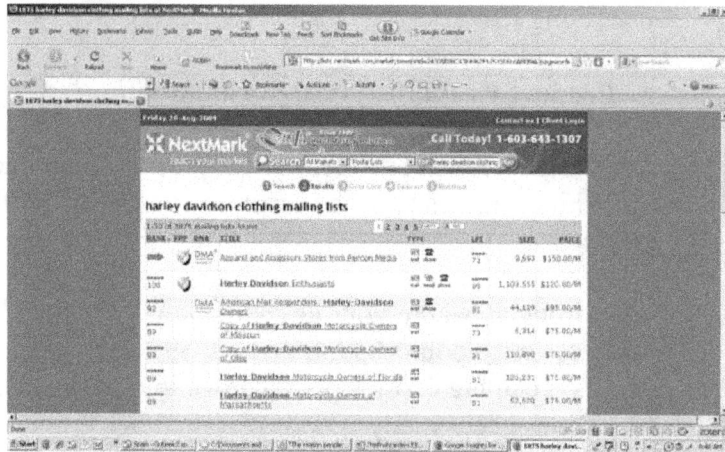

Now anything with the word "enthusiast" in it is well worth looking at so click on this list.

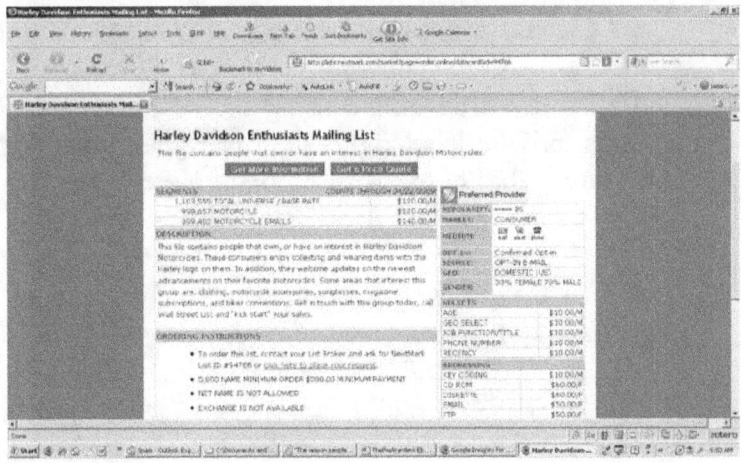

What you see above is called a datacard. A datacard is a full description of a mailing list.

🔵 Total number of names on list (also called the total universe).

🔵 New people on list (also call the hotline).

🔵 Suggested Usage - types of advertisers that have rented this list in the past.

🔵 Different selects - you pay an additional select cost for additional stats, i.e. age, income.

🔵 How list was generated? By mail is best.

🔵 Buy magazines of the market you want to use to get an idea of what is being sold.

🔵 Conduct Internet searches using Google and Google Insights.

🔵 Info Products - Produce the products yourself or paying someone to write a course.

🔵 Use Elance, Rentacoder, Guru, Freelance, etc. to outsource this type of work.

License a product from someone that has produced one.

Do a search online using the search terms: Resale rights, private label rights, reprint rights. Look for sales resources that come with product. Here are some that I use:

http://www.master-resale-rights.com/
http://www.plrebooks.co.uk/
http://www.sallys-ebooks.co.uk/
http://www.floodle.net/
http://www.freeebooksonline.org
http://7dollaroffers.com/
http://www.tradebit.com/

Estimating - cost to produce, lead time to produce.

Digital product vs. hard product: Harder to return hard product, lower chargebacks!

NOTE: Do not produce product until market is tested to see if it sells first.

4. The Fundamentals of the Mailing List...

Picking a list is the most important aspect of postcard marketing – I use http://www.Nextmark.com.

You can also use Standard Rates and Data Service (SRDS) - Direct Marketing Lists - Public libraries usually have these.

Mailing List characteristics to look for:

Want a list with decent size and hotline numbers.

84

Datacards: Universe - Total number on list.

Hotline Numbers - new additions to list or # of people that purchased within last 30-days.

Summary Description - describes buyers and how they got on the list. What did they buy and how does it match up with what you are selling? How did they buy? How much did they spend?

Best list is a list that is direct mail generated.

Do you recognize the company renting the list?

Read all the datacards on the market you have chosen so you can find the closets match to your product.

Call list broker to determine any info about list. Also call the list manager.

List owner > list managers > list broker

List brokers can and will direct you to their lists because they do not share commissions with list manager.

To prevent this: Have more than one broker or compare notes between list managers, owners, and make sure what list broker is telling you the right info.

How to find a list broker: you want someone with experience, someone you can get along with and will work with a new person.

How long in the business?

How long have they been brokering?

Why are they renting list?

What is their specialty or expertise? Use Google!

99% of the time list is one time only.

Lists
re seeded so they know if you used it more than once!

What are terms - COD, Net 30, etc?

What is the turnaround time for lists?

Continuation —Very important…how many companies have rented this list have come back and rented it again?

Most lists have 5,000 minimums. Three types of list to use:
Buyers List
Responders List (responded to an offer asking for more info)
Compiled List (phonebook)
Reduced price if you buy whole universe ONLY after you have tested list in your market.

Here are some list brokers to try:

http://www.1000lists.com/
http://www.findlists.com/
http://www.allmediainc.com/
http://www.keenote.com/
http://www.martinworldwide.net/

5. The Design, Layout, and Printing of the Postcard…

A postcard is not designed to sell anything, but it is designed to get a customer to take an action…push 1 and a phone message describes the entire offer. This is where the sale occurs.

Layout: Think in terms of classified ads - Short, sweet, and to the point.

The headline - the more specific the better: "Drive a golf ball farther than you ever have before!"

The body copy is two to three sentences or paragraphs.

Call to action: For more information call our toll free 24-hr recorded message.

Check out Google AdWords ads; look at these headlines for Harley Davidson clothing (see below).

Notice the AdWords ads in the right hand column. Short and sweet and to the point!

Sponsored Links

Harley Merchandise
Authentic **Harley** Coins for
your Hog Rider. Many Designs
HarleyCoins.com
Harley Davidson Clothes

87

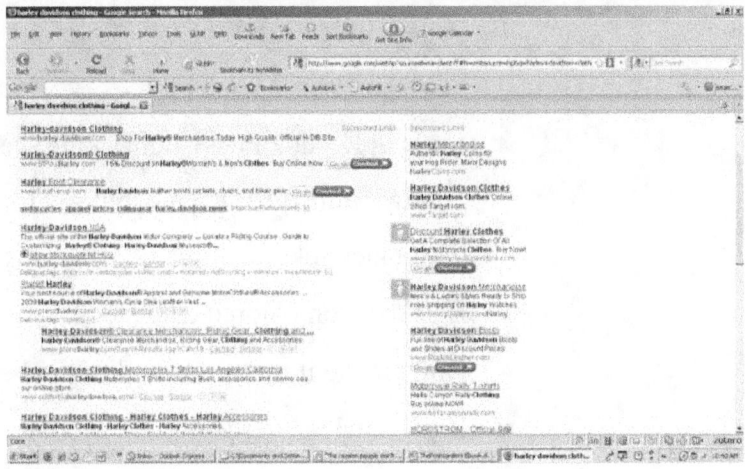

Use eye-catching headlines like: "Who Else Wants to Make $859/day?", "We've been trying to reach you!"

Postcard Layout Template:

- Headline
- Body
- Call to action
- 800 toll free number

Here is where I get my toll free numbers and operators to take my orders:

Kall8: http://tollfree.kall8.com/14539.htm

- Size: big postcards are not worth it. 4 x 6 is best.

- Paper: Index stock 65#; 110# cover stock (card stock).
- Use ugly colors - light pink, canary yellow, mint green, pale blue card stock with black ink.
- Black ink on colored card stock.
- Don't make it pretty; the uglier the better.
- Horizontal vs. vertical - be different.
- Stay away from graphics; only text unless graphics are compelling.
- Two sided; address side is a code number that operator can ask for so you can track what list was used.
- Or after the phone number use extension # or is your code number for program #4.
- No return address on the card.
- Mail big volume use bulk mail.
- Lettershop mails and addresses.
- Sales message and list are the most important aspects of this program.

Example #1

HOW TO OVERCOME FINANCIAL MELTDOWN

Has someone stolen your time, talents and energy in return for some low paying wage or salary?

Has someone stolen your peace and well-being as you stress over your current financial condition?

Has Someone Stolen YOU?

* We can help! We will teach you everything!
* No hype or gimmicks! No inflated income claims!
* No selling or multi-level marketing!
* It will cost you an investment of less than $100!
* It takes about 2-hours/day! Check it out...

www.StealingYou.com

Example #2

How to overcome financial meltdown

Has someone stolen your time, talents and energy in return for some low paying wage or salary?

Has someone stolen your peace and well-being as you stress over your current financial condition?

6. The Recorded Sales Message...

This is your sales call or you recorded audio call to action. It is also known as a verbal sales letter. I want to make you aware of a resource I use extensively. It is the book, "The Ultimate Sales Letter" by Dan Kennedy. Since you will be writing these scripts and recording your own sales message, I strongly advise you to get this book.

In it, Kennedy describes one scenario he calls "Problem - Agitation – Solution". He has another scenario called "Fortune Telling". Another of his scenarios is called "The Winners 5%/The Losers 95%". I would concentrate on learning these three scenarios because they will teach you how to write effective and compelling scripts.

The length of the sales message should be from 1.5 minutes - 7 minutes: whatever it takes to sell the product. Short messages do not work as well as long messages, and mine average about 4.5-5 minutes.

Should price be in the recorded message? Sometimes the price should be in the recorded message and sometimes it should be in the closing call depending if the operator doesn't have sales skills. If the operator does not have sales skills then put the price in the recorded message.

Use your own voice and not a professional voice over unless the arena is high class stuff like golf, etc.

Include the phrase - Press 1 at any time.

Work on the urgency! "When was the last time you didn't worry about monthly bills?"

Don't use scarcity copy! The FTC considers this scammy. Scarcity copy is something like this, "There are only 50 copies available so don't delay…order now!"

Strong and powerful guarantee is mandatory! ALWAYS provide a money back guarantee.

Use testimonials if you can get them and they sound genuine and real.

If you use Kall8, http://tollfree.kall8.com/14539.htm then you are provided an auto-attendant where you can record your sales call over the phone or upload a .wav file. I prefer you record the sales message and upload a .wav file.

Here is some excellent **free** recording software that you can download from Audacity. Study the analytics given by Kall8 and see if the campaign is working or discover why it is not.

7. The Operator Closing Call…

When testing, take the calls yourself instead of paying for an operator. Remember: this is only a test of a 1000 postcard mailing.

Upsell on the Closing Call whenever possible.

You can find some interesting upsell items here:

AsSeenOnTVNetwork
http://www.asseenontvnetwork.com/

Here is a sample script to give you an idea:

Hi, this is operator #507.My name is John. May I please have your code number on the bottom left hand corner of your card?

Thank you and may I have your name please?

Thank you, Chris, and just to let you know this call may be recorded for quality assurance, okay?

Where would you like your package shipped to please? (Verify back to customer).

And your phone number please?

With your permission, Chris, may we check in from time-to-time to check on your progress? Is that okay?

Okay great. The best way to do that is with email. May I have your email address please?

And to get the package mailed out to you today we can use a credit or debit card. Which do you prefer? Okay, great.

What is name as it appears on the card?

What is the card number?

What is the expiration date?

Is your billing address the same as your shipping address?

Great! Your package will be delivered by mail within the next 5-7 business days.

Your card will be charged $69 plus $10 S&H for a total of $79 even.

Thank you for calling and have a great day.

8. Testing Your Campaign...

Most of the time your campaign will fail the test! Does this sound strange to you? It shouldn't; remember postcard marketing is all about the law of numbers. The 1000 postcard tests are designed to find only the products that you can sell in huge amounts. Most, if not all, of your tests will be profitable but the ones that demonstrate huge profits are the ones you want to let rip.

Two types of testing in a Push 1 system

Initial Testing determines if the project is viable and worth pursuing.

Long Term Testing tests different elements to improve numbers you have already received.

Initial testing comes before any inventory is purchased or anything is done at all.

95

Test two versions of a postcard - different style, different headline, same call to action.

Put different tracking code - three digit extension or in left hand corner.

Use different codes for lists and postcards - track every single element.

If new in the market, get most responsive list from list broker.

250 sheets of card stock make 1000 postcards. A test = 1000.

Merge names onto the postcards - 4-Up at Kinkos.

Merge Excel file to a Word doc. Saved as a PDF take to copy shop like Kinkos or Staples.

Buy 1000 stamps and mail them.

Record message on auto-attendant then Press 1 to you, to a voice-mail, or to a cheap call center.

Best days for mailing are Thursday, **Friday**, and Saturday.

Tests measure how many people responded to the postcard, 7-8% response/1000 postcards. Second, test the actual recorded message. Third, how many that pressed 1 actually ordered.

Untrained phone room 40-50% close ratio.

Don't fall in love with the deal!

Is length of message too long or too short? Tone of voice?

Ask friends to give you feedback.

Woman's or man's voice? Women are best.

Price point?

Offer vs. price are not the same.

Only test one element at a time.

Push 1 rates can be as high as 25%.

Pyramiding your profits - pay for growth out of profits. Let project pay for itself. START SLOW!

5000 piece mailing to start.

As you raise the amount of your mailings, the numbers will go down. You make it up in volume.

Important metrics to watch:

- The number of people calling from the postcard
- The number of people pushing 1
- The number of people ordering

Number of returns is critical! Normal return rate is 6-9%

Front loading a list: gives you the most responsive on your first purchase while subsequent buys to the same list draws zip.

When you order you want an Nth count, which takes names throughout the list. Doesn't apply to hotline lists.

9. Understanding the Costs...

It goes without saying that you should always keep your costs low. When conducting tests, I use companies like Staples and Kinkos to print (they use high speed copiers and not printers and then cut the cards for me) the cards and mail merge the mailing lists names and addresses. I then place the postage on each card. I do this for my 1000 postcard tests.

Here is a list of costs you should always be aware of no matter how big or how small the campaign is:

- Postcard Design and Graphics
- Postcard Printing
- Cost of Mailing List
- Mail Merge Names and Addresses
- Postage
- Call Center Push 1 Service and Operator Service
- Merchant Account Fees

http://www.paypal.com
http://www.bankcardusa.com/

http://www.1shoppingcart.com/

● Cost of Product
●Cost of Fulfillment

http://www.thefulfillmenthouse.com/
http://www.speakerfulfillmentservices.com/
http://www.cftech.com/BrainBank/MARKETING/Direc-
RespFulfil.html
http://www.innotrac.com/?gclid=CKCizLPMyZwCFR0S
agod8hsoKA

10. Completely Automate the Whole Program

Go here: http://click2mail.com.
Open an account.
Click on Download Template.
Click on Postcards.
This is the one you want:

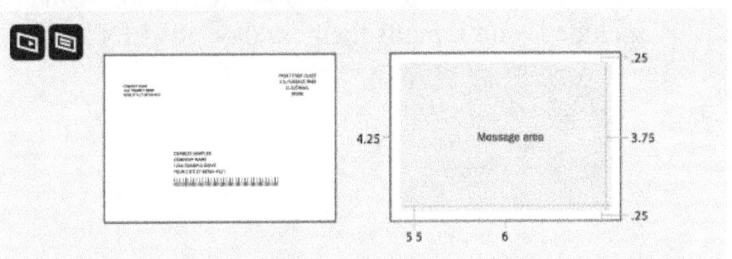

PC21 Postcard, regular (SpaceSaver), 6 x 4.25 in, printed one-side
PRINTING one-side, black and white or 4-color (full color)
PAPER   4-color 80 lb. cover, white, uncoated

80 lb. cover, white, gloss, UV coating one-side

black & white 65 lb. cover, yellow, uncoated

80 lb. cover, white, uncoated

POSTAGE First-Class (estimated delivery: 2-4 days)

International First Class (estimated delivery: 7-30 days)

Postcard product sheet (PDF: 1.25 MB)
PC21 - Postcard Word Template (DOC: 27.50 KB)

All you have to do is design the postcard like Example #2 above,

Upload your mailing list.

Pay for it (as low as 30-cents/1000 with printing included) and it mails the next day. SWEET!

Chapter 9 - Books to TV

http://voyagemedia.com/

I only use Voyage Media Group when I am turning a book into a TV program. They are the best, but they are not cheap!

You will work closely with an industry executive or producer   experienced
in your project's genre, and with other experts who bring specialized
industry skills. The Voyage Media Professionals Program team   members
have expertise and track records in all areas of the industry.

- Studio & Independent Film

- Scripted Television

- Branded Content & Transmedia

- Documentaries

- Reality TV

For writers
- Strategy for creating a concept with commercial appeal
- Script notes from TV or film executives
- Guidance in approaching representation

Voyage Media is a turnkey, all-encompassing company. They literally do it all for the author. So check them out!

Chapter 10 - Fast TV Exposure

Television as a Mass Medium Rocks!

Television is not the ultimate mass medium; but it is one that delivers profitability consistently if used correctly. It is not as pervasive as it used to be and over the past two decades, it can easily be said that, like the car manufacturers, it has shot itself in the foot.

Do you remember when there were a few car brands such as Mercedes-Benz and Cadillac that were high end luxury brands? Now, there are so many brands that are high end that the status symbol has diluted to a point where just about every car is high end.

In television programming the same situation has occurred. There are too many channels and people are unhappy because the content has become less creative and imaginative. We seem to be stuck in "reality show hell" and forced to watch commercials about feminine douches and feminine napkins.

Like cars, our choices may be many but our options are fewer.

Yes, there are high ranking shows and micro-audiences that faithfully watch because they have similar interests. These are called affinity viewers. Affinity viewers are important, and we will talk more about these later.

Everything from automotive to beauty has an immense following, which enables an advertiser better targeting abilities.

The gluttony of channels and markets provide a very unique advantage to advertisers of all types products and services. Packaging various markets at very low per spot prices has changed the way advertisers buy media. We will also talk about packaging later on in this book.

Included in this mix is the combining of ad mediums to achieve the maximum PUNCH. I will demonstrate combining strategies in order to demonstrate these advantages.

Next, I will present the types of TV advertising that are available and the ones you should use based on your product and service.

Personally, I use TV advertising to sell my books. I am a self-published author with over 200books on Amazon.com alone. I combine email advertising with TV advertising to move thousands of books per month. Email and television is a marriage made in heaven.

I am going to show you how I do this and the resources I use to accomplish a high 5-figure income per month.

There are many different types of commercials and packages to employ these resources. In this book, I will concentrate on "cheap spots" and low price point products and services.

Whether you are a self-published author, own a small brick and mortar business, or possibly own a home-based business, this chapter will show you how to skyrocket your sales.

So let's get at it and get you on your way to profitability…

Have a Plan and a Budget!

PLAN FIRST!

Don't even think of beginning without a plan in place. Planning is the most important part of television exposure.

The first part of your plan is to determine what the goal is before you begin to achieving that goal. It is not enough to say, "I want to make money." That is the effect and your plan NEEDS to have the cause in it.

The first thing you should know about your plan is to factor in consistent long term advertising when dealing with TV or radio. Results DO NOT HAPPEN OVERNIGHT and like many forms of advertising, you must build a brand of consistency and trust before seeing any returns on investment. The upside potential is so enormous with TV advertising that it is worth the expense and time in building this brand.

The American Marketing Association (AMA) defines a brand as a "name, term, sign, symbol, or design, or a combination of them intended to identify the goods and services of one seller or group of sellers and to differentiate them from those of other sellers".

Companies or products need to have an edge that makes them stand out from the crowd, something that makes them more appealing and interesting to the customer or consumer. Branding aims to establish a significant presence in the market that attracts customers.

A good media group will help you to create a unique name, logo, and image design for your products, goods, or services if you don't have one or it is poor. Then they employ a cost effective television and radio advertising campaign with a consistent theme, reach, and frequency to create public awareness and demand.

The second thing is to produce top-quality commercials and to **TEST, TEST, TEST** everything. Don't skip this step and then wonder why your investment isn't paying off. Why show something to an audience that doesn't like what it is seeing and hearing? If we did this in dating, there would be no marriage and no kids and mankind would be extinct.

Seriously, I have seen time and time again advertisers sending out the same commercial that has been demonstrating diminishing returns just because it is marginally profitable and they are too lazy to invest in another commercial or do a better job.

Please don't do this; we have enough garbage on TV now, and we cannot risk losing any more viewership.

Next – demographics - your plan should outline in detail the demographics of your target audience. Your media buyer will ask so be prepared to give it in detail.

There are two types of campaigns:

1. Ad Campaigns
2. PR Campaigns

PR Campaigns involve a Press agent/publicist and are used to get interviews on various programs. These are also called personal appearances.

Public Relations provides an organization access to their audiences utilizing topics of public interest and news items to shape customers, investors, and the general public's view or perspective. A Public Relations specialist's job is anticipating, analyzing, interpreting, and generating public opinion, attitudes, and issues that might impact, for good or ill, the operations and plans of the organization.

Planning and implementing the organization's communications efforts and influencing change in public opinion or reputation are achieved through an arsenal of media tools. In every tactic– whether it is launching a new product or service with a media blitz, holding a press conference, annual reports, direct mail, a visual identity program, website marketing, or a social networking program, your media team should be focusing on key marketing objectives.

You will need a good publicist, and I have listed one below:

Yvonne Hudson
412-512-0589
yvonne@newplace.us

Lynette Asson
412-973-9828
lynette@newplace.us

If you opt for #2 then you will need to get good at being in front of a camera and doing interviews. Believe me; it is considered an art form. You will not believe how poorly you will come across initially.

Budget – without a doubt the most important aspect of any ad campaign! DO NOT run a one-time only campaign and expect results. It won't happen, and it is nonrealistic. If you need help on budgeting then speak with your media buyer. Here is a great one:

Mia Compomizzi
Television Ad Group
Office: 212.844.9057 x506
Fax: 724-728-2454
mia@televisionadgroup.com
http://www.televisionadgroup.com

Your product demographics will tell you where to run your ads and on what channels. Above all else, speak with Mia and get the facts.

Producing a Viable TV Commercial

Commercials and Video Trailers Can Go Viral

Video is powerful; so powerful that people would rather watch than read. Here are some videos I have used to increase my book business and business in general:

21st Century Marketing Genius Demo
http://youtu.be/UhAiPT675ms

21st Century Marketing Genius Book
http://youtu.be/YiPDvZ-khOc

Applied Mind Sciences
http://youtu.be/XiL26mH8zFE

BookbuilderPLUS
http://youtu.be/oUfwolfxK1E

Confessions of a Child Predator
http://youtu.be/26_gJiJ7nTo

Getting Rid of Cellulite in 10-Days
http://youtu.be/vCl767qUnrc

Drop 3-Dress Sizes in 30-Days
http://youtu.be/ZRdq142crc0

Effective Email Advertising
http://youtu.be/MMkqRTCXssA

Embarrassing Problems Fix
http://youtu.be/bE2mda4qDus

Energy Psychology
http://youtu.be/HQZcS1u_s6s

ePubWealth Program
http://youtu.be/c53yYgeRosA

ForensicsNation Commercial
http://youtu.be/DfnMfkM08-U

FreebiesNation Blueprint
http://youtu.be/pLzyw98fThg

How to Write a Kindle Book in Hours
http://youtu.be/9ew-REgRr80

Publish with A Purpose
http://youtu.be/OP2BvPJGc7c

The Power of Observation
http://youtu.be/LueSxfL3awI

You Can Run But You Cannot Hide
http://youtu.be/X7qt6PEkohA

Commercials and Videos are inexpensive to produce and
effectively get across any message you choose to submit

to the viewer. Once the video is produced, you may post it on over 200-video sharing sites for maximum exposure. Here is a list of sites I use:

http://www.ebaumsworld.com/
http://www.spike.com/
http://break.com/
http://www.metacafe.com/
http://www.atom.com/
http://www.veoh.com/home.html
http://vodpod.com/tag/grouper
http://www.Dailymotion.com
http://www.Blip.tv
http://www.screencast.com/
http://wooshii.com/
http://www.zillatube.com./
http://www.slideshare.net/
http://www.screenr.com/
http://robo.to/
http://www.flixya.com
http://www.uvouch.com
http://www.magnify.net/sites/categories
http://www.ulinkx.com/
http://www.myvidster.com
http://www.gemzies.com/
http://www.infectiousvideos.com/
http://www.videosift.com
http://www.vewgle.com
http://www.tagged.com
http://www.wonderhowto.com
http://http://www.maxior.pl
http://www.nowpublic.com
http://www.vodpod.com

http://www.kontraband.com
http://www.ttr2.co.uk
http://www.flabber.nl
http://www.abum.com
http://www.voomed.com
http://www.beautyandthedirt.com
http://www.boredjunk.com
http://www.directgamez.com
http://www.myarcadespot.com
http://www.godofhumor.com
http://www.prankies.com
http://www.jabers.com
www.ridiculousvideos.com
http://www.dumbr.com
http://www.pan-fun.com
http://www.shockthis.com
http://www.exbyte.net
http://www.vidaxs.com
http://www.boredtown.com
www.milkandcookies.com
http://www.theaffiliated.net/
http://www.boxee.tv/
http://www.brightroll.com/
http://www.dailymotion.com/us
http://www.desksite.net/
http://www.hulu.com/
http://www.mefeedia.com/
http://www.red-lever.com/
http://www.revver.com/
http://www.scanscout.com/
http://eyespot.com/
http://crackle.com/
http://jumpcut.com/

http://ourmedia.org/
http://vimeo.com/
http://www.vsocial.com/
http://www.tremormedia.com
http://www.vibrantmedia.com/
http://www.vidcat.com/
http://www.videoegg.com/
http://www.vidsense.com/
http://vlaze.com/
http://www.volomedia.com/
http://www.yumenetworks.com
http://video.yahoo.com/
http://vids.myspace.com/
http://video.msn.com
http://video.aol.com/
http://www.heavy.com/
http://video.google.com/
http://www.tubemogul.com
http://www.youtube.com/
http://imageshack.us/
http://yfrog.com/
http://www.viddler.com
http://www.adhysteria.com
http://www.bofunk.com
http://www.esnips.com
http://www.guba.com
http://www.iviewtube.com
http://www.kewega.com
http://www.livevideo.com
http://www.megavideo.com
http://www.motionbox.com
http://www.photobucket.com
http://www.sharkle.com

http://www.u2upfly.com
http://www.vidilife.com
http://www.viddyou.com
http://www.screencast.com/pricing.aspx

Commercials are one thing and videos are another. Commercials are the point of sales part of the equation and videos reinforce the sale.

Video does more than just provide viewers with entertainment and content; video also establishes credibility and trust.

One of the most effective ways to produce video and get people to watch is humor. Funny videos sell, and they sell consistently. Humor keeps bringing people back for more. Think about the baby commercials that eTrade runs or some of the IHOP commercials. People love funny and humorous commercials, and they consistently rate high among all age groups.

In my book, "Distraction Marketing" I teach that sex, humor, and fear distract the viewer's attention and get them to pay attention to your stuff. When producing your own videos, keep in mind that although sex, humor, and fear sell, content is still king and the content you produce should tell a story and get people to go visit your landing page and/or website or call a toll-free number to order.

I have a saying – "Tell then Sell!" Think about this for a moment: what commercials and videos do you enjoy and why? I will bet hard money that the ones you enjoy best are the ones that tell a story and that make you feel some kind of emotion.

The hype ones you recognize quickly as hype and your mind will tune them out unless it is a product or service you need and/or are interested in.

It is important to remember that planning your commercial/video is important insofar as what the stated goal is and also remember, you only have either 30-seconds or 60-seconds to get your message across.

Selling books is one thing and quite different than selling beauty salon services. You have a different targeted audience, a different call to action, and a different price point.

For example, my books are priced from $2.99-$9.97 in PDF format. My gross profit is the price of the book since they are digital downloads with zero fulfillment cost. If the customer orders the paperback or Kindle version, Amazon handles the fulfillment and not me.

The minimum run I do for a book is $2,000 in commercial spots which translates into a good many commercials, the amount of which depends on the markets I am running in.

But for example's sake, let's assume I received 2,000 spots for $2,000.

In order to break even, I would have to sell over 200 books. Now that seems like a lot, and it is, but the

116

minimum I sell is always more than 700 books so it is quite profitable.

No, I didn't achieve these figures right out of the box. I had to fine-tune my commercials and test various markets but now this is pretty consistent.

The commercial production costs were about $500 so you can see TV promotion is quite lucrative.

Buying Cheap TV Spots

Package 1
Runs any channel anywhere any time of day
Runs across 1 million homes
400 commercials
Runs across 2 week period
$500

Package 2
Runs any channel anywhere any time of day
Runs across 4 million homes
Minimum 1500 commercials
Runs across a 2 week period

117

$1000

Package 3
Runs any channel anywhere any time of day
Runs Across 4 million homes
Minimum 2500 commercials
Runs across a 3 week period
$2000

Package 4
Runs any channel anywhere any time of day
Runs across 5 million homes
Minimum 5000 spots
$2500

Prices may vary so talk to
Mia Compomizzi
Television Ad Group
Office: 212.844.9057 x506
Fax: 724-728-2454
mia@televisionadgroup.com
http://www.televisionadgroup.com

Very few television viewers have not been exposed to
television commercials. Commercials might attempt to

sell products, support certain politicians, or increase public awareness and, often, they helped shape popular culture and succeed in both engaging and defining audiences.

Commercial ads date back to the 1450s and became popular with the invention of the printing press. In colonial America, advertisements were particularly popular in stores and print media.

The nature of advertising evolved as technology increased. Radio provided auditory marketing and target marketing using demographics. Television provided a moving image to create even more effective and memorable advertisements.

The average child watches over 20,000 commercials in a single year. The average American adolescent will see 360,000 television commercials before graduating from high school. By the age of 65 years, the average person will have seen 2 million television commercials.

There are three kinds of television commercials:

- Product or brand marketing, public service announcement and campaign advertisement.

- Product/brand marketing commercials are intended not only to sell specific products but to increase brand loyalty among consumers.

- A public service announcement is a message to increase awareness about social issues, and it often sways audiences in a certain direction.

Television has provided controversy and most of the controversy surrounding television commercials has involved advertisements that promote the use of potentially dangerous products, such as cigarettes and alcohol.

Advertising agencies have been accused of targeting children and adolescents with such ads.

The introduction of digital video recorders (DVRs) has posed some problems for traditional television advertising because viewers can fast-forward through commercials, bypassing ads.

To combat DVRs, product placement has become more popular. Product placement is a technique in which companies pay for certain products and brands to be featured within the set or story of a television show so that viewers are still exposed to their products.

The Federal Trade Commission regulates all TV ads, and their guidelines state that advertisers who make a claim that their product or services perform better or are preferred over others must be able to substantiate the claim.

The average cost of a TV ad is between $13 and $60 per spot. The cost varies depending on time of day it is run and the length of the ad, which can be15, 30, or 60 seconds long.

Advertising cost depends on the programming. According to EconomicExpert.com, a 30-minute show will have approximately 12 minutes of commercials, while a 60-minute show will have approximately nine minutes of commercials.

Here are 7 reasons why this is so, plus supporting evidence and links:

- TV is one of the best profit generators.
- TV facilitates brand memories for goods and services.
- People watch an hour more of commercial TV a week than 10 years ago.
- TV and not the Internet is the dominant youth medium.
- The latest new technologies allow people to watch more TV.
- TV is a point of sale medium.
- TV is the most discussed ad medium.

The PWC Payback Study 1

- TV pays back an average 4.55 times in increased sales; 30% more than press.
- TV delivers almost the same value (80%) to the brands in the year following any investment as in the year of investment itself.
- TV is the most effective generator of brand value and what distinguished the brand value leaders in

every market we studied was a dominant TV share of voice.

The PwC Payback Study 2

- If brands cut their TV advertising budget, there is a 73% chance of damaging brand value; but if brands increase investment in TV, and there is a 67% chance of increasing brand value.

The IPA Study

- Campaigns focusing on fame and emotion were far more effective in driving the bottom line (sales, market share, profit, and loyalty) than more rational campaigns based on information and persuasion.
- TV was the most efficient medium at increasing market share in relation to share of voice.
- TV is getting more effective over time; it has increased its lead over all other media channels in each of the last three decades.
- TV advertising remains one of the most effective and efficient forms of media.
- TV is typically processed at a low involvement level, which means the content is less critically analyzed but this makes it well suited to thematic or brand messages that need to be remembered for the long-term. Information which enters the memory through low involvement processing gets stored directly via the emotional centers of the brain straight to the long-term, implicit memory without any conscious filtering.

- TV is an incredibly effective way of increasing a set of associations around a brand. It literally hardwires brands into the brain.
- **fMRI** scans demonstrate that the two parts of the brain most stimulated when watching audio-visual material (like TV and cinema) are the amygdala (emotion) and the hippocampus (long term memory encoding). Emotions and long term memory = where brands live. Neuroscience studies from a variety of media companies (Viacom, GMTV, and PHD) have confirmed this finding. The work of Professor Robert Heath on low involvement processing is worth reading.

Video Production
Low Cost TV Ads
http://lowcosttvads.com/
Jeff Neill
JN Productions/Low Cost TV Ads
jnprod@pobox.com
jeffneill@lowcosttvads.com
972-317-7225
888-MYTVADGUY

Media Buyer
Television Ad Group
http://www.televisionadgroup.com/

Mia Compomizzi
Office: 212.844.9057 x506
Fax: 724-728-2454
mia@televisionadgroup.com
www.televisionadgroup.com

SMS Platform
Twilio
http://www.twilio.com/

Mobile Ad Networks
http://www.3cinteractive.com/
http://www.4th-screen.com/
http://www.admob.com/
http://www.adultmoda.com/
http://www.admoda.com/
http://www.admob.com/
http://www.amobee.com/main/hp.htm
http://www.apptera.com/
http://www.buzzcity.com/
http://lat49.com/
http://www.free411.com/
http://www.google.com/mobileads/
http://www.greystripe.com/
http://web.hands.com.br/home
http://www.hipcricket.com/
http://www.hothand.com/
http://advertising.apple.com/
http://inmobi.com/
http://www.jumptap.com/
http://www.madhouse.cn/en/
http://www.mads.com/
http://lat49.com/

http://www.millennialmedia.com/
http://advertising.microsoft.com/mobile
http://www.mojiva.com/
http://www.puddingmedia.com/
http://advertising.yahoo.com/adsolution#product=Mobile
http://www.ybrantmobile.com/
http://en.group.yoc.com/

Chapter 11 - Appendix of Advertising & Marketing Resources

Ad Networks

http://www.adconion.com/
http//www.adecn.com/
http://www.adify.com/
https://amp.admarketplace.com/
http://www.adready.com/
http://adsoftheworld.com/
http://www.adtegrity.com/
http://www.advertising.com/
http://www.adzacta.com/
http://www.amperemedia.com/
http://www.axill.com/
http://www.burstmedia.com/
http://www.casalemedia.com/
http://www.collective-media.com
http://www.connexuscorp.com/

http://www.cpxinteractive.com/
http://www.crucialinteractive.com
http://www.dedicatednetworks.com
http://easyad.org/
http://www.etology.com/
http://www.federatedmedia.net/
http://innovationinteractive.com/
http://leadermarkets.com/
http://www.marketrated.com/
http://www.mediawhiz.com/
http://www.motiveinteractive.com/
http://www.oridian.com/
http://www.platform-a.com/
http://www.precisionclick.com/
http://www.pubmatic.com/
http://www.quadrantone.com/
http://www.redmccombsmedia.com/
http://www.rightmedia.com/
http://www.smartchannelmedia.com/
http://www.specificmedia.com/
http://www.teracent.com/
http://www.theblindnetwork.com/
http://www.ttzmedia.com/
http://www.turn.com
http://www.undertone.com/
http://www.valueclickmedia.com/
http://vantagemedia.com/
http://www.vizi-inc.com/

Ad Swaps
http://www.imadswaps.com
http://www.warriorforum.com/warrior-joint-ventures/

Analytics
http://chartbeat.com/
http://www.reinvigorate.net/
http://www.haveamint.com
http://www.woopra.com
http://www.getclicky.com
http://piwik.org/
http://www.kissmetrics.com/
http://www.goingup.com/
http://www.engineready.com/
http://www.stuffedtracker.com/
http://www.crazyegg.com/
http://awstats.sourceforge.net/
http://www.markosweb.com/

Answers Marketing
http://www.amswers.com/
http://www.linkedin.com/answers
http://www.mahalo.com/answers/
http://answers.yahoo.com/

Apps
http://www.apple.com/iphone/apps-for-iphone/
http://www.android.com/market/#app=com.com2us
http://developer.apple.com/iphone/index.action
http://www.crowdspring.com/
http://www.coroflot.com/
http://www.adwhirl.com/
http://www.magmito.com/
http://www.appmobi.com/
http://www.conduit.com/
http://ibuildapp.com/
http://imified.com/

http://portableapps.com/

iTunes
http://www.apple.com/itunes/affiliates/download/
http://itunes.apple.com/linkmaker
http://www.youtube.com/music

Article Sites
http://www.myarticlenetwork.com/
http://www.articlepostrobot.com
http://www.articlez.com/
http://www.articledude.com/
http://arborgroup.org/MetaFilterTrick/
http://www.articlemarketer.com
http://www.goarticles.com
http://forums.digitalpoint.com
http://ideamarketers.com/
http://www.articledashboard.com/
http://www.buzzle.com/
http://articlepower.free.fr/index3.html
http://www.articledistribution.com/
http://www.amazines.com/
http://www.articlesnatch.com/
http://www.articleforfree.com/
http://www.articlesbase.com/
http://www.articlecity.com/
http://articlealley.com/
http://ezinearticles.com/
http://www.articlesubmitter.imwishlist.com/
http://www.submityourarticle.com/
http://www.humanspinner.com/
http://articleclick.com/

Audio
http://audacity.sourceforge.net/
http://nextvoice247.com/
http://www.apple.com/itunes/podcasts/specs.html
http://www.podcast411.com/page2.html

Authority Sites
http://bravejournal.com/
http://www.dailymakeover.com/
http://www.livejournal.com/
http://www.metafilter.com/
http://www.xanga.com/
http://www.squidoo.com
http://www.huppages.com
http://www.gather.com/
http://www.xanga.com/

Autoresponders
AWeber: http://www.aweber.com/?284935
GetResponse: http://www.getresponse.com/

-
Backlinks
http://howismysite.com/
http://www.weberlinks.com/
http://freebacklinkcheck.com/
http://ismysiteindexed.com/
http://markosweb.com/
http://backlinksindexer.com/
http://linklicious.me/
http://www.dripfeedblasts.com/
http://www.commentkahuna.com
http://www.neurolinker.com/
http://www.linkvana.com/

http://www.neurolinker-linkvana-deal.com/
http://www.buildmyrank.com/
http://www.linkmaster.com/
http://www.linkerage.com/
http://www.linktrackr.com/offer/
http://www.textlinks.com/
http://www.bruteforcelinkingloophole.com/
http://atniz.com/dofollow-blog-commenting-services/
http://www.onewaytextlink.com/links.php?type=free
http://www.majesticseo.com/
http://home.snafu.de/tilman/xenulink.html
http://atniz.com/dofollow-blog-commenting-services/
http://bloglinkgeneratorpro.com/
http://adage.com/power150/
http://www.pjsqualitybacklinks.com/

BackUp
http://www.mediamax.com/

Banners
http://www.bannersmall.com/
http://www.click4click.com/
http://www.exchangead.com/
http://www.impressionz.com/uk/
http://bannerpie.com/
http://exchangebanners.net/
http://www.freebannernetwork.com/
http://www.hit4hit.co.uk/
http://www.bannerco-op.com/join/
http://www.adversharing.com/
http://www.exchangead.com/index.html
http://www.hitx.net
http://www.linkbuddies.com/

http://www.lotofstuffs.com/index.php
http://www.backbonebanners.com/index.php
http://www.ms-links.com/
http://www.yfwbannerexchanger.com/join.asp
http://www.exchange-it.com/
http://home.free-banners.com/
http://5000banners.com/

Behavioral Networks
http://www.adaptlogic.com/
http://www.claria.com/
http://www.criteo.com/
http://www.frontporch.com
http://www.interclick.com/
http://www.leiki.com/
http://www.nebuad.com/
http://www.nugg.ad
http://www.phorm.com/
http://www.prudsys.com/
http://www.revenuescience.com/
http://www.tacoda.com/
http://www.tattomedia.com/
http://www.wunderloop.com

Bid Networks
http://www.adbidcentral.com
http://www.bid4spots.com
http://www.bidvertiser.com/
http://www.mediabids.com
http://www.quigo.com/

Blog - Google "Guest Blog"
http://blogcarnival.com/bc/

http://www.theblogsolution.com/howitworks/
http://www.bloggersblog.com/blognetworklinks/
http://esapps.com/blogcarnival/index.php
http://www.mbpninjaaffiliate.com/
http://www.networkedblogs.com/
http://www.commenthut.com
http://www.commentkahuna.com
http://www.blogcommentor.com/
http://answers.yahoo.com/
http://www.wikihow.com
http://www.blogburst.com/
http://www.blogbooker.com/
http://pajamateam.com/
http://www.levorsoft.net

Blog Ad Networks
http://www.blogads.com/
http://www.blogowogo.com/
http://www.creative-weblogging.com/
http://www.reviewme.com/

Blogging Sites
http://www.Blogger.com
http://www.Wordpress.com
http://www.Livejournal.com
http://www.Vox.com
http://www.Tumblr.com
http://www.Clearblogs.com
http://www.Blog.com
http://www.Thoughts.com
http://www.Blogster.com

Blog Commenting

http://arborsupport.com/howtolinks/16-DofollowBlogComments1/index.html
http://www.commentkahuna.com/

Blog Communities
http://spicypage.com
http://MyBlogLog.com
http://www.blogcatalog.com

Blog Marketing
http://9rules.com/
http://www.blogbooker.com/
http://gawker.com/
http://w.networkedblogs.com/
http://pajamateam.com/

Blog Search
http://www.icerocket.com/

Bookmarking Sites
http://www.autosocialposter.com/
http://www.delicious.com/popular
http://digg.com
http://www.feedshot.com
http://socialmarker.com/
http://socialblaster.com/
http://www.socialmatic.com/
http://www.socialposter.com/
http://www.onlywire.com/
http://www.submisocial.com/
http://bookmarkingdemon.com/
http://www.warrichpk.com/manual-social-bookmarking.php

http://keotag.com/

Boutique Ad Networks
 http://diningdialog.com/
http://www.adheremedia.com/
http://www.adsportsfocus.com/
http://www.animaladnetwork.com/
http://www.e-healthcaresolutions.com/
http://solutions.focalex.com
http://www.glammedia.com/
http://www.healthline.com/
http://www.hispanoclick.com/
http://www.jumpstartautomotive.com/
http://www.markethealth.com/
http://www.marthastewart.com/marthas-circle
http://www.sportgenic.com/
http://www.waterfrontmedia.com/
http://weather.weatherbug.com/
http://adnetwork.ymexchange.com/

Brainstorming
http://www.ideaengine.org/

Buy Websites
http://marketplace.sitepoint.com/
http://www.viperbusiness.com/listings/
http://www.flippa.com

Classified Ads
http://www.usfreeads.com/
http://dir.yahoo.com/Business_and_Economy/Classifieds
?skw=yahoo+classifieds
http://www.supershopper.org/

http://www.afcp.org/
http://www.mediauk.com/
http://www.kijiji.com/
http://www.microfieds.com/success5564
http://www.myspace.com/index.cfm?fuseaction=disabled
http://www.epage.com/
http://www.yelp.com/la
http://www.national-classifieds.com/
http://www.adicio.com/
http://www.backpage.com
http://www.cityamerica.com/
http://www.citynews.com/
http://www.tnol.com/
http://www.craigslist.org/
http://www.inetgiant.com/
http://www.livedeal.com
http://www.merchandiseselect.com
http://www.nationwideadvertising.com/
http://www.usnetads.com/
http://walmart.oodle.com/

Classified Ad Search Engine
http://www.Oodle.com

Cloaker (link)
http://www.nullrefer.com/

College Advertising
http://www.campusmediagroup.com/
http://www.alloymarketing.com/
http://www.campusclients.com/

Content

http://www.articles-written.com
http://www.associatedcontent.com/
http://www.congoo.com/
http://www.need-an-article.com
http://www.contentdivas.com/
http://www.webmarketingnow.com/
http://www.work.com/
http://www.marketing-referral-tools.com/marketing-tools.php

Content Aggregators
http://www.9rules.com/about/join/

Content Farms
http://www.answerbag.com/
http://www.associatedcontent.com/
http://www.demandmedia.com/

Content Syndication
https://www.istockanalyst.com/login
http://www.momsnetwork.com/submit-articles.shtml
http://www.newscom.com/nc/showMainNCPage.action
http://www.ning.com/
http://pligg.com/
http://sta.rtup.biz/
http://pubsub.com/

Contextual Ad Networks
http://www.adgenta.com/
http://www.adagencypro.com
http://www.contextual-advertising.org/
http://www.industrybrains.com/
http://www.brand.net/

http://chitika.com/
http://www.clicksor.com/
http://www.contextualmarketplace.com/
http://www.contextweb.com/
http://www.drivepm.com/
http://www.expoactive.com/
http://fairadsnetwork.com/
http://www.google.com/intl/en/ads/
https://www.kanoodle.com/about/brightads.html
http://www.kontera.com/
http://www.mediatext.com/
http://www.modernclick.com/
http://www.namimedia.com/
http://www.personifi.com/
http://www.quigo.com/
http://www.realtechnetworks.com/
http://www.targetpoint.com
http://publisher.yahoo.com/
http://www.ValidClick.com
http://www.pulse360.com

Conversion
http://www.conversionchronicles.com/

Cool Sites of the Day
http://www.coolsiteoftheday.com
http://selfmademinds.com/200703/100k-site-history-
november-2005-first-1000/
http://www.linkingmatters.com/2004/09/cool_site_of_the
_day
http://picks.yahoo.com/
http://www.topsiteoftheday.com/
http://www.askmen.com/daily/sites/2009/09/index.html

http://www.blackstump.com.au/anew.htm
http://www.familyfirst.com/

Co-Registration Services:
http://www.ftc.gov/bcp/conline/pubs/buspubs/canspam.sh
tm
http://www.permissiondata.com/
http://www.coregmedia.com
http://opt-intelligence.com/
http://www.multiplestreammktg.com/
http://www.national-leads.com/
http://listbuilderpro.com/

Coupon Submission Sites
http://www.supercoolcoupons.com/
http://www.couponcabin.com/
http://www.ultimatecoupons.com/
http://www.freeshipping.org/
http://www.dealtaker.com/forums.html
http://spreadsheets.google.com/pub?key=p4bAsllwd0Fl
MmPng37LvTA
Find Customers and Backlinks by Adding Your Site to
Coupon Directories

CPA Networks
https://portal.advaliant.com/Affiliate/New_AffEditProfile
.aspx?Signup=1&ReferralID=4530
http://partners.cpacoreg.com/signup/CD4947
https://my.clickbooth.com/signup/CD54363
http://www.lynxtrack.com/afclick.php?o=5831&b=y301c
m4r&p=14&s=18459-120x60
http://www.incentreward.com/refjoin.php?affiliate_id=C
D6049

http://leadermarkets.com/signup/CD10609
http://affiliates.millnicmedia.com/signup/CD9834
http://www.pjtra.com/t/QTxFQEBIPEZAREg8QkRE
http://rextopia.com/signup/CD8775
http://www.shareresults.com/t/xmlbuilder.php?mid=105&sid=16355&cid=14129

Create Your Own Home Page
http://www.google.com/ig?hl=en

DataFeeds
http://aws.amazon.com/
http://blogprofitz.com/
http://www.datafeedr.com/
http://ezseonews.com/general/dig/

Digg/Social Elves
http://www.SocialElves.com

Document Automation
http://www.drawloop.com/
http://www.pdf2pageturn.com/
http://www.pdftokindle.com/
http://www.epagewizdrm.com/
http://www.epagewiz.com/
http://www.ecatalog.com/
http://www.ebrochures.com/
http://www.dnldrm.com/

Domain
http://www.dnscoop.com/
http://www.namestation.com/
http://www.domainsbot.com/

Download Portals
http://dropbox.com
https://www.payloadz.com/
http://www.downloadpipe.com/
http://www.digitaldeliveryshoppingcart.com/?
http://home.plimus.com/ecommerce/
http://www.rapidspread.com/
http://www.tradebit.com/
http://www.carbonite.com/en/
http://www.filesanywhere.com/
http://www.9down.com/
https://upload.cnet.com/

Duplication
http://www.discmakers.com/

Email
https://hypermail.acunett.com/cart.php
http://www.rhinoemailer.com
http://www.email-marketing-power.com/
http://www.expedite-email-marketing.com/index.htm
http://mailchimp.com/

Exclusive Products Listings
http://7dollaroffers.com/?e=support@neternatives.com
http://www.click2sell.eu/
http://www.master-resale-rights.com/
http://www.worldniche.com/

Ezine
http://www.directoryofezines.com/
http://www.swapezineads.com/

http://www.ezinehits.com/ad-rates.htm
http://www.cashfromhome.com/solo.html
http://www.superpromo.com/optadorder.html
http://www.ProBizTips.com/advertising.html
http://www.unimaxmarketing.com/powerpak.html
http://www.flashyads.com/advertise.html
http://topliving.com/marketing/fmailing.htm
http://www.marketingtrendz.com/advertising.htm
http://www.premieroptin.com/

Free Fax
http://faxzero.com/

Forum
http://www.boardtracker.com/
http://boardreader.com/
http://www.forumtrafficgold.com/?rid=52
http://www.promojunkie.com/
http://www.howtocorphelp.com/htforum/
http://ablakeforum.com/index.php
http://www.wickedfire.com/
http://omgili.com/
http://www.warriorforum.com/forum/
http://www.dealtaker.com/forums.html
http://www.webmasterworld.com/
http://ForumFind.com
http://Big-Boards.com
http://www.ivillage.com/messageboards?ice=iv,mp,rn,mb
http://messages.yahoo.com/
http://moneycentral.msn.com/community/message/

Franchise
http://www.bizwits.com/

Free Ads Companies
http://www.free-advertising-blog.com/
http://www.thefreeadforum.com
http://business.blinkweb.com/

Freeware
http://www.techsupportalert.com/

Game Networks
http://www.doublefusion.com/
http://www.igaworldwide.com/
http://www.massiveincorporated.com/
http://www.mochimedia.com/

Google
http://www.google.com/blogsearch
http://www.google.com/addurl/?continue=/addurl
www.google.com/ads/innovations/
http://books.google.com/
www.google.com/calendar
www.google.com/adplanner/
http://www.google.com/cse/?v
http://www.google.com/friendconnect
http://www.google.com/events/io/2011/index-live.html
http://www.google.com/insights/search/#
http://www.google.com/trends
https://adwords.google.com/select/KeywordToolExternal
http://www.google.com/merchants
http://www.prchecker.info/check_page_rank.php
http://www.google.com/places/
http://www.google.com/intl/en/press/zeitgeist/index.html
http://www.google.com/intl/en_us/products/submit.html

https://profiles.google.com/
http://www.google.com/tools/firefox/suggest/
http://video.google.com/
http://wave.google.com/
http://www.google.com/webelements/
http://www.google.com/webmasters/
http://www.google.com/zeitgeist
http://www.google.com/ig?aig=0&reason=1
http://www.google.com/websiteoptimize
http://www.correlate.googlelabs.com/
http://maps.google.com/
http://www.google.com/mobile/
http://www.google.com/mobile/search/
http://images.google.com/imghp?hl=en
http://video.google.com/?hl=en
http://translate.google.com/?hl=en
http://groups.google.com/grphp?hl=en
http://knol.google.com/k?hl=en
http://www.google.com/patents?hl=en
http://www.google.com/prdhp
http://docs.google.com

Groups Marketing
http://groups.google.com/
http://groups.yahoo.com/

Headline Analyzer
http://www.aminstitute.com/headline/index.htm

Hosting
HostMonster: http://tinyurl.com/6wfctcm $5.95/month
HostGator: http://bit.ly/30Hcv0 7.96/month
Hostzilla: http://tinyurl.com/7k42bz2 $5.95/month

MochaHost: http://tinyurl.com/7tdlt2r $7.43/month
iPower Hosting: http://tinyurl.com/cd4d52f $5.95/month
HostNine: http://tinyurl.com/cmw56pq **$3.95/$6.95**
Dedicated ip
TMD Hosting: http://tinyurl.com/7ux55zv $3.85/month
IX Web Hosting: http://tinyurl.com/79ujby7$7.95/month
WinHost $9.95/month
NameCheap Hosting $3.95/$7.45/$13.95
CoolHandle $3.95
http://www.lunarpages.com/ $19.95
http://order.1and1.com/ $6.99
http://www.bluehost.com/ $5.95
http://www.seohosting.com/
http://hitdirector.com/ dedicated servers

Image Marketing Sites (Free Pics and Photos Rights)
http://www.public-domain-photos.com/
http://imagebase.davidniblack.com/
http://www.freephotosbank.com/
http://www.freejpg.com.ar/
http://www.cepolina.com/freephoto/
http://visipix.dynalias.com/index_hidden.htm
http://www.burningwell.org/gallery2/main.php
http://tofz.org/
http://stock.diwiesign.com/
http://www.unprofound.com/
http://www.freefoto.com/
http://amygdela.com/stock/
http://www.zurb.net/zurbphotos/
http://energy.star29.net/store/
http://www.photogen.com/
http://www.sxc.hu/home

In-Image Ad Sites
http://www.pixazza.com/ is now
http://www.luminate.com
http://gumgum.com/
http://www.thinglink.com/
http://stippleit.com/
http://shopsense.shopstyle.com/page/ShopSenseHome
http://www.hyperspots.com/
http://www.clikthrough.com/
http://www.imagespacemedia.com/

International Networks
http://www.b5media.com/
http://www.mediosone.com
http://www.oridian.com

Joint Venture
http://v3.jvnotifypro.com/account/
http://jvnotifypro.amplify.com/
http://www.jointventurefinder.com/
http://www.nichechoppers.com/

Keyword
http://www.mikes-marketing-tools.com/adwords-wrapper.html
http://www.goodkeywords.com/
http://www.traffictravis.com
http://www.jumbokeyword.com/
http://www.keyworddensity.com/
http://www.keyworddiscovery.com/
http://www.ispionage.com/
http://www.keywordspy.com
http://www.spyfu.com/

http://www.terapeak.com/
https://freekeywords.wordtracker.com/
http://tools.seobook.com/keyword-tools/seobook/
http://www.kwbrowse.com
http://www.quintura.com
http://www.nichebotclassic.com/

Keyword Monitoring
http://alp-uckan.net/free/monitorthis/

Landing Pages
http://addictomatic.com/
http://www.yourbizwebsites.com/global5618

Literary
http://www.araloc.com/mobile?gclid=CKrnyeqtoaoCFYc
aQgodGTVCXg
https://authorcentral.amazon.com/gp/landing
http://www.drawloop.com/solutions/
http://www.fatnoggin.com/
http://www.suite101.com/
http://www.rightstracker.com/
http://www.scribd.com/
http://www.scribd.com/mobile
http://www.isbn.org/standards/home/index.asp

Local
http://www.adzzoo.com/
http://www.everyblock.com/
http://www.everyscape.com/
http://happn.in/sponsor
http://www.localconnex.com/
http://pritzer.com/

http://www.thebluebook.com/
https://www.thumbtack.com/
http://www.transvertise.com/
http://www.yell.com/
http://www.yodle.com/learn-more/

Marketing Tools
http://www.mikes-marketing-tools.com/free-marketing-tools.html

Mindmap
http://freemind.sourceforge.net/wiki/index.php/Main_Page

Mobile Ad Networks
http://www.3cinteractive.com/
http://www.4th-screen.com/
http://www.admob.com/
http://www.adultmoda.com/
http://www.admoda.com/
http://www.admob.com/
http://www.amobee.com/main/hp.htm
http://www.apptera.com/
http://www.buzzcity.com/
http://lat49.com/
http://www.free411.com/
http://www.google.com/mobileads/
http://www.greystripe.com/
http://web.hands.com.br/home
http://www.hipcricket.com/
http://www.hothand.com/
http://advertising.apple.com/
http://inmobi.com/

http://www.jumptap.com/
http://www.madhouse.cn/en/
http://www.mads.com/
http://lat49.com/
http://www.millennialmedia.com/
http://advertising.microsoft.com/mobile
http://www.mojiva.com/
http://www.puddingmedia.com/
http://advertising.yahoo.com/adsolution#product=Mobile
http://www.ybrantmobile.com/
http://en.group.yoc.com/

Mobile Content Sites
http://www.mofuse.com/
http://www.mobisitegalore.com/

Mobile CPA Networks
http://www.offermobi.com/
http://www.sponsormob.com/en/
http://peerfly.com/?r=13154
http://www.ewanetwork.com/
http://www.mobiklix.com/
http://applied5564.mobpartner.com/
http://www.mundomedia.com/
http://affiliates.tattomedia.com/
http://www.wolfstormmedia.com/
http://365adsolutions.com/

Mobile Online Tools
http://www.mobilemonopoly.com/membersonly-secret-
tool-secruity-access101/
http://www.offermobi.com/webinar/list/
http://www.offermobi.com/page/tools/

http://www.pixdrop.com/
http://www.coolutils.com/Online/Image-Converter/
http://www.testiphone.com/
http://iphonetester.com/
http://bango.com/live/default.aspx
http://www.fonefinder.net/
http://www.onetruemedia.com/
http://animoto.com/
http://www.mobilemonopoly.com/secret-tool/

Mobile Outsourcing
http://www.replacemyself.com/
http://123employee.com/
http://www.econsultant.com/
http://www.elance.com/
http://www.agentsofvalue.com/
http://www.guru.com/index.aspx
http://www.rentacoder.com/
http://www.scriptlance.com/
http://www.allfreelance.com/
http://www.agentsofvalue.com/
http://www.microworkers.com/
https://www.odesk.com/w/?_redirected
http://www.skillwho.com/
http://www.contentnetwork.com/
http://www.warriorforum.com/warriors-hire/
http://www.getafreelancer.com

Mobile Search Engines
http://www.google.com/mobile/
http://www.taptu.com/corp/
http://mobile.yahoo.com/search
http://www.discoverbing.com/mobile/

Mobile SMS Texting Platforms
http://www.tellmycell.com Albert at 212 255-7029 ext
215
http://www.esendex.us
http://www.message-media.com

Music
www.PumpAudio.com (Len's Favorite)
http://www.acidplanet.com
http://www.royaltyfreemusic.com
http://www.wavtracks.com
http://www.premiumbeat.com
http://www.ibaudio.com
http://www.musicbakery.com

Niche
http://www.di66.net/

Organize
http://www.iprioritize.com/
http://www.web-appointments.com/
http://www.xobni.com/
http://www.timetrade.com/
http://astrid.com/
http://www.jaiku.com/
http://www.ideastorm.com/
http://www.spoke.com/

Other Resources
http://www.aweber.com/?284935
http://www.roboform.com/php/pums/rfprepay.php?affid=
ta556

http://www.vflyer.com
https://getyowza.com/
http://www.kelleydrye.com/index
http://www.advertisinglawyer.ca/

Pay Per Call Networks
http://www.ringrevenue.com/
http://www.cj.com/
http://www.shareasale.com/
http://quakemarketing.com/
http://www.marchex.com/
http://www.ingenio.com/
http://www.ringrevenue.com/
http://www.upsnap.com/
http://paypercall.attinteractive.com/ m
http://www.flyingspider.com/
http://www.upaypercall.com/
http://services.google.com/advertisers/us/media/mobilead
vertising

Pay Per Click
http://www.google.com/AdWords
https://adcenter.microsoft.com/
http://marketinginfo.yahoo.com/contactForm/
http://www.miva.com/
http://www.looksmart.com/

Pay Per View (PPV or CPV) Resources
http://corporate.adonnetwork.com/
http://www.clicksor.com/
http://www.directcpv.com/
https://www.leadimpact.com/
http://www.mediatraffic.com/

152

http://www.trafficvance.com/
http://www.megaclick.com/
http://www.icewatermedia.com/
http://www.zango.com

PPV Networks
http://www.hydragroup.com/
http://www.neverblue.com/
http://www.cxdigitalmedia.com/
http://www.copeac.com/

Pay Portals
http://budurl.com/c9h5
http://bango.com/
http://www.billingrevolution.com/
http://www.blingnation.com/
http://www.boku.com/
http://www.paybycheck.com
http://www.billmelater.com
https://www.xoom.com/
https://www.paypalobjects.com/IntegrationCenter/ic_mic
ropayments.html

Photography
http://www.gettyimages.com/?country=usa
http://www.istockphoto.com/index.php
http://www.istockphoto.com/video
http://www.jupitermedia.com/
http://photobucket.com/
http://www.wireimage.com/

Pics-Photo

http://www.picturetrail.com/photoFlick/samples/acrobatc
ube/l_acrobatcube.shtml
http://www.sliderocket.com/
http://rockyou.com/ry/home
http://www.slide.com/
http://www.photographersindex.com/
http://www.picresize.com/
http://mypictr.com/
http://snipshot.com/

Ping Sites
http://autopinger.com/
http://blo.gs/ping.php
http://www.pingoat.com/
http://ping.fm/
http://www.pingler.com/
http://pingomatic.com/
http://www.weblogs.com/
http://pingates.com/
http://pingfarm.com

Podcast Networks
http://www.apple.com/business/podcasting/
http://www.clickz.com/3578416
http://www.gigadial.com/public/
http://www.podcastingnews.com/tag/podcast-networks/
http://www.arbornetworks.com/podcasts
http://www.thepodcastnetwork.com/
http://www.podcastalley.com
http://www.podcastdirectory.com

PPD
http://www.drawloop.com/solutions/

http://gtrafficpumpsystem.net/system/index.php
http://www.scribd.com

Press Release-Title must have keywords
http://www.PRWeb.com
http://www.1800pressrelease.com
http://www.1888pressrelease.com
http://www.i-newswire.com
http://www.pr.com
http://www.publicityinsider.com
http://www.wikihow.com
http://www.publicityhound.com/
http://www.prleap.com/
http://www.prlog.org/
http://www.ducttapemarketing.com/instant-press-release#_%20blank
http://www.ereleases.com/
http://www.helpareporter.com/
http://www.prleads.com/

Public Domain
http://www.abebooks.com/
http://www.alibris.com/
http://www.bartleby.com/
http://buyoutfootage.com/
http://www.gutenberg.org/wiki/Main_Page
http://www.filmchest.com/
http://emol.org/movies/
http://www.ibiblio.org/
http://www.archive.org/details/movies
http://www.oclc.org/us/en/global/default.htm
http://www.publicdomaintorrents.net/
http://www.kickbuttideas.com/pd/

http://www.readprint.com/

Public Multisites
http://www.wordpress.com
http://www.blog.com
http://wwwhostablog.net
http://blogetery.com/

Public Relation Firms
http://emsincorporated.com/
http://www.hotguest.com/
http://www.businesswire.com/portal/site/home/
http://www.prnewswire.com/

Readers
http://www.pluck.com/
http://www.google.com/reader

Research Platforms
http://www.quantcast.com/
http://www.alexa.com/
http://www.google.com/insights/search/#
http://www.google.com/trends
http://correlate.googlelabs.com/
http://www.google.com/press/zeitgeist.html
http://groups.google.com
http://catalogs.google.com
http://www.plentyoffish.com/demographicInterests.aspx
https://siteexplorer.search.yahoo.com/mysites
http://www.trendwatching.com
http://www.trendhunter.com
http://www.lipsticking.com/
http://www.trendsight.com/

http://50.lycos.com
http://pulse.ebay.com
http://www.coolshopping.com
http://www10.shopping.com/top_searches
http://hotsearches.aol.com
http://www.craigslist.com
http://del.icio.us/popular
http://www.magazines.com
http://www.amazon.com/exec/obidos/tg/browse/-/599858/
http://www.yureekah.com/
http://marketplace.clickbank.net
http://sem.smallbusiness.yahoo.com/searchenginemarketing/ or
http://advertising.microsoft.com/searchadvertising.
http://www.consumersearch.com

RSS Feeds
http://www.rssfeedssubmit.com/?hop=1aw2bt
http://www.mass-automation.com/index.php
http://www.rss-ground.com/?hop=allenjess
http://Feedster.com
http://Technorati.com
http://IceRocket.com
http://Google.com/blogsearch
http://Blogpulse.com
http://home.spaces.live.com/
http://news.yahoo.com/
http://news.google.com/
http://www.bing.com/news
http://Newsgator.com
http://Bloglines.com
http://www.allscoop.com/rss-submit.php

http://www.pjsqualitybacklinks.com/
http://www.rssmix.com/
http://pipes.yahoo.com/pipes/
http://www.blogoculars.com/
http://www.2rss.com/
http://www.rssfeeds.com/
http://www.plazoo.com/
http://www.page2go2.com/
http://www.rssmicro.com/
http://www.feedfury.com/
http://www.rssmountain.com/
http://www.findrss.net/
http://www.feedbase.net/
http://www.rssmotron.com/
http://www.daytimenews.com/
http://www.rss-feeds-submission.com/
http://www.millionrss.com/
http://www.readablog.com/
http://www.goldenfeed.com/
http://www.blogdigger.com/
http://www.feed24.com/
http://www.weblogalot.com/
http://www.feedboy.com/
http://www.chordata.info/
http://www.blogpulse.com/
http://www.blogpulse.com/
http://www.icerocket.com/
http://www.rss-network.com/
http://www.jordomedia.com/
http://www.feeds2read.net/
http://www.feedshark.brainbliss.com/
http://www.feedplex.com/
http://www.feedcat.net/

http://www.rssmad.com/
http://www.feedage.com/
http://www.newsisfree.com/
http://www.syndic8.com/
http://www.newzalert.com/

Screen Capture
http://goview.com/
http://www.techsmith.com/jing/

Sell-Ads Companies
http://www.Etology.com
https://www.adbrite.com/
http://www.adengage.com/sellads.cfm
http://www.adjungle.com/
http://www.adsbay.co.uk/
http://www.adspace-auctions.com/
https://www.adster.com/
http://bannergarage.com/
http://www.emptyspaces.eu/
https://www.text-link-ads.com/
http://www.clickagents.com/
http://itsyourad.com/
http://www.valueclickmedia.com/
http://buysellads.com/
http://sharethis.com/
http://bit.ly/aSwLkt

Seminar Archive
http://hardtofindseminars.com/

SEO
http://www.ambergreeninternetmarketing.co.uk/

http://www.boostability.com/free-site-submission/
http://www.pagerankplace.com/addurl.html
http://www.seoquake.com/
http://www.trafficapple.com/
http://www.traffictravis.com/
http://www.internetmarketingninjas.com/tools/
http://www.quirk.biz/searchstatus/
http://analyticsdigger.org/

Short URLs
http://www.adjix.com/
https://bitly.com/
http://budurl.com/
http://longurl.org/
http://realurl.org/

Social Media Ad Platforms
http://www.youtube.com
http://www.facebook.com/advertising
https://www.myads.com/login.html
http://www.plentyoffish.com/advertising.aspx
http://www.adcause.com/
https://www.stumbleupon.com/pd/index/redirect-ads/
https://www.linkedin.com/ads
http://boo-box.com/?locale=en-US

Social Media Tools
http://www.trackur.com/
http://gold.insidenetwork.com/facebook-marketing-bible/
http://www.insidefacebook.com/2007/12/09/inside-facebook-marketing-bible-24-ways-to-market-your-brand-company-product-or-service-in-facebook/
http://www.meebo.com/

Social Networks
http://www.digg.com
http://www.delicious.com
http://www.socialelves.com

Split Test
http://www.splittester.com/
http://www.zentester.com/

Startups
http://www.killerstartups.com/
http://sta.rtup.biz
http://www.startupnation.com/

Submission Sites
http://www.9rules.com/
http://www.addurl.nu/
http://alltop.com/submission/
http://www.directorysubmits.com/
http://www.warrichpk.com/orderpage.php
http://www.linksmaster.com/
http://www.submitcentre.com/
http://www.dmoz.org/
http://populair.eu/
http://www.seocompany.ca/directory/top-web-directories.html

Telemarketing
http://www.globalsky.com/
http://www.outbounders.com/
https://www.donotcall.gov/

Text Link Ads
http://www.Text-Link-Ads.com
http://www.TextLinkBrokers.com

Track changes on web pages
http://www.copernic.com/en/products/tracker/index.html
http://www.aignes.com/
http://watchthatpage.com/

Tracking & Metrics
http://bango.com
http://www.hitsconnect.com/
http://www.tracking202.com/home
http://www.adtrackz.com/
http://www.clicktale.com/
http://www.getclicky.com/
http://www.hypertracker.com/

Tutorial Sites
http://www.Instructables.com.
http://www.noupe.com/
http://www.tutorialized.com
http://www.epinions.com
http://www.good-tutorials.com/
http://www.pslover.com/
http://www.pixel2life.com/
http://www.tutorialsphere.com/
http://www.tutorialkit.com/
http://www.rnel.net/
http://toxiclab.org/
http://tutorial-index.com/
http://designbump.com/
http://www.designfloat.com/

http://www.photoshoproadmap.com/
http://www.tutorials-expert.com/
http://www.cg-links.com/
http://www.fstutorials.com/
http://tutorialoutpost.com/
http://www.tutorialsgarden.com/
http://psd.tutsplus.com/
http://psdtop.com/
http://graphic-design-links.com/
http://design-newz.com/submit-newz/
http://woork.blogspot.com/2009/02/add-design-news-on-woork.html
http://devmarks.com/
http://www.dzone.com/
http://www.1stwebdesigner.com/contribute/
http://www.tripwiremagazine.com
http://www.webdesignbooth.com/
http://www.crazyleafdesign.com/blog/contributors/
http://psdlearning.com/
http://www.brushking.eu/submit_news.php
http://kailoon.com/
http://www.myinkblog.com/submit-news/
http://www.fuelyourcreativity.com/user-link-feed/
http://designm.ag/submit-news/
http://www.flashperfection.com/submit.html
http://www.tutorial-center.com/submit/
http://www.totaltutorial.com/
http://www.designshard.com/contribute/
http://www.knowtebook.com/publish
http://sharebrain.info/submit/
http://www.photoshop911.com/tutorial.html
http://www.cg-links.com/submit-link.php
http://www.tutorialsgarden.com/submit/

http://www.v7n.com/graphics/submit.php
http://www.tipclique.com/
http://gfxtuts.com/
http://www.tutorio.com/
http://designmoo.com/
http://www.zabox.net/
http://www.knowthis.com/

Validation
http://validator.w3.org/
http://www.authenticatedtestimonials.com/
http://www.validatedsite.com/

Video Sharing
http://www.ebaumsworld.com/
http://www.spike.com/
http://break.com/
http://www.metacafe.com/
http://www.atom.com/
http://www.veoh.com/home.html
http://vodpod.com/tag/grouper
http://www.Dailymotion.com
http://www.Blip.tv
http://www.screencast.com/
http://wooshii.com/
http://www.zillatube.com./
http://www.slideshare.net/
http://www.screenr.com/
http://robo.to/
http://www.flixya.com
http://www.uvouch.com
http://www.magnify.net/sites/categories
http://www.ulinkx.com/

http://www.myvidster.com
http://www.gemzies.com/
http://www.infectiousvideos.com/
http://www.videosift.com
http://www.vewgle.com
http://www.tagged.com
http://www.wonderhowto.com
http://http://www.maxior.pl
http://www.nowpublic.com
http://www.vodpod.com
http://www.kontraband.com
http://www.ttr2.co.uk
http://www.flabber.nl
http://www.abum.com
http://www.voomed.com
http://www.beautyandthedirt.com
http://www.boredjunk.com
http://www.directgamez.com
http://www.myarcadespot.com

http://www.godofhumor.com
http://www.prankies.com
http://www.jabers.com
www.ridiculousvideos.com
http://www.dumbr.com
http://www.pan-fun.com
http://www.shockthis.com
http://www.exbyte.net
http://www.vidaxs.com
http://www.boredtown.com
www.milkandcookies.com
http://www.theaffiliated.net/
http://www.boxee.tv/

http://www.brightroll.com/
http://www.dailymotion.com/us
http://www.desksite.net/
http://www.hulu.com/
http://www.mefeedia.com/
http://www.red-lever.com/
http://www.revver.com/
http://www.scanscout.com/
http://eyespot.com/
http://crackle.com/
http://jumpcut.com/
http://ourmedia.org/
http://vimeo.com/
http://www.vsocial.com/
http://www.tremormedia.com
http://www.vibrantmedia.com/
http://www.vidcat.com/
http://www.videoegg.com/
http://www.vidsense.com/
http://vlaze.com/
http://www.volomedia.com/
http://www.yumenetworks.com
http://video.yahoo.com/
http://vids.myspace.com/
http://video.msn.com
http://video.aol.com/
http://www.heavy.com/
http://video.google.com/
http://www.tubemogul.com
http://www.youtube.com/
http://imageshack.us/
http://yfrog.com/
http://www.viddler.com

http://www.adhysteria.com
http://www.bofunk.com
http://www.esnips.com
http://www.guba.com
http://www.iviewtube.com
http://www.kewega.com
http://www.livevideo.com
http://www.megavideo.com
http://www.motionbox.com
http://www.photobucket.com
http://www.sharkle.com
http://www.u2upfly.com
http://www.vidilife.com
http://www.viddyou.com
http://www.screencast.com/pricing.aspx

Video Embedding Sites
http://www.WonderHowTo.com
http://www.flixya.com
http://www.spike.com
http://www.instructables.com
http://www.myspace.com
http://www.uvouch.com
http://www.magnify.net/sites/categories
http://www.ulinkx.com/
http://www.gemzies.com/
http://www.infectiousvideos.com/
http://www.videosift.com
http://www.vewgle.com
http://www.tagged.com
http://www.wonderhowto.com
http://http://www.maxior.pl
http://www.nowpublic.com

http://www.myvidster.com
http://www.ning.com
http://www.vodpod.com
http://www.mefeedia.com

Voice Overs
http://www.voices.com/
http://VoiceTalentNow.com
http://www.provoiceusa.com
http://amazingvoicetalent.com
http://www.provoiceusa.com

Web 2.0 Blog Sites
http://atwiki.com/
http://blog.com/
http://blogabond.com/
http://blogcheese.com/
http://blogetery.com/
http://blogger.com/
http://blogladder.com/
http://blogr.com/
http://blogsome.com/
http://blogspirit.com/
http://blogster.com/
http://blogyx.com/
http://bloki.com/
http://bravenet.com/
http://busythumbs.com/
http://calameo.com/
http://clearblogs.com/

Web 2.0 Sites
http://www.Squidoo.com

http://www.Hubpages.com
http://www.tumblr.com
http://www.blogger.com
http://www.Scribd.com
http://www.Zimbio.com
http://www.Wetpaint.com
http://www.wordpress.com
http://www.Instablogs.com
http://www.Weebly.com
http://www.Blogsome.com
http://www.Xanga.com
http://www.wikispaces.com
http://www.Blinkweb.com
http://www.Wikidot.com
http://www.Twine.com
http://www.Docstoc.com
http://www.Knol.google.com
http://www.Slideshare.net
http://www.Ehow.com
http://www.Quizilla.com
http://dairlyland.com/
http://easyarticles.com/
http://easyjournal.com/
http://etribes.com/
http://freevlog.com/
http://friendster.com/
http://gather.com/
http://goarticles.com/
http://greatestjournal.com/
http://home.spaces.live.com/
http://insanejournal.com/
http://isnare.com/
http://jimdo.com/

http://livejournal.com/
http://multiply.com/
http://netcipia.com/
http://nexo.com/
http://ning.com/
http://onsugar.com/
http://opendiary.com/
http://scribd.com
http://shoutpost.com/
http://sites.google.com/
http://sosblog.com/
http://soulcast.com/
http://squarespace.com/
http://terapad.com/
http://thoughts.com/
http://tooum.com/
http://tripod.com/
http://trippert.com/
http://ufem.com/
http://webs.com/
http://wordcountjournal.com/
http://xanco.com/
http://zoomgroups.com/
http://zoomshare.com/

Web Check
http://www.onlinewebcheck.com/
http://siteexplorer.search.yahoo.com/
http://tools.seobook.com/backlink-analyzer/
http://www.backlinkwatch.com/
http://www.fonefinder.net/
http://iphonetester.com/
http://www.testiphone.com/

http://blog.grader.com/
http://www.blogpulse.com/tools.html
http://namechk.com/
http://tweet.grader.com/
http://www.backlinkwatch.com/
http://www.whatismyip.com/
http://www.websiteoptimization.com/services/analyze/
http://validator.w3.org/docs/checklink.html
http://www.ip-adress.com/
http://www.geobytes.com/IpLocator.htm?GetLocation
http://www.aminstitute.com/headline/index.htm
http://tools.seobook.com/general/keyword-density/
http://www.internetmarketingcourse.com/freeheadlinegenerator/
http://www.dlguard.com/dlginfo/index.php
http://tools.seobook.com/backlink-analyzer/
http://www.compete.com/
http://www.freesticky.com/stickyweb/
http://www.paessler.com/tools/psi/
http://www.iwebtool.com/tools/
http://www.ranks.nl/tools/spider.html
http://www.virustotal.com/
http://www.webmaster-toolkit.com/
http://www.wesquare.com/

Website Builders
http://www.yourbizwebsites.com/index_orig2.php
http://your-mini-site-creator.com/index.php
http://www.yola.com/
http://www.wix.com/
http://www.weebly.com/
http://www.websnapr.com/
http://www.webstarts.com/live-domains.php

http://www.we-b-sites.com/
http://www.webs.com/
http://www.snowcovered.com/Snowcovered2/Default.aspx
http://www.igroops.com/
http://www.squarespace.com/
http://internet-business-world.com/myfreewebsitebuilder.html
http://www.instantsqueezepagegenerator.com/
http://www.oswd.org/

Written Resources
http://mmaglobal.com/?q=node/1851
http://www.mobilemarketer.com/
http://www.mobilemarketingmagazine.co.uk/
http://www.mmaglobal.com/bestpractices.pdf
http://mobithinking.com/mobile-ad-network-guide
http://www.cellphone-advertising.com/
http://www.thinkaction.com/

Word of Mouth Marketing
http://mylikes.com/
http://www.extole.com/
http://izea.com/
http://sponsoredtweets.com/
http://socialspark.com/
http://wereward.com/
http://inpostlinks.com/
https://payperpost.com/
https://www.reviewme.com/

I Have a Special Gift for My Readers

I appreciate my readers for without them I am just another author attempting to make a difference. If my book has made a favorable impression please leave me an honest review.   Thank you in advance for you participation.

My readers and I have in common a passion for the written word as well as the desire to learn and grow from books.

My special offer to you is a massive ebook library that I have compiled over the years. It contains hundreds of fiction and non-fiction ebooks in Adobe Acrobat PDF format as well as the Greek classics and old literary classics too.

In fact, this library is so massive to completely download the entire library will require over 5 GBs open on your desktop.

Use the link below and scan all of the ebooks in the library. You can select the ebooks you want individually or download the entire library.

The link below does not expire after a given time period so you are free to return for more books rather than clog your desktop. And feel free to give the link to your friends who enjoy reading too.

I thank you for reading my book and hope if you are pleased that you will leave me an honest review so that I can improve my work and or write books that appeal to your interests.

Okay, here is the link…

http://tinyurl.com/special-readers-promo

PS: If you wish to reach me personally for any reason you may simply write to mailto:support@epubwealth.com.

I answer all of my emails so rest assured I will respond.

Meet the Author

Dr. Leland Benton is Director of Applied Web Info, a holding company for ePubWealth.com, a leading ePublisher company based in Utah. With over 21,000 resellers in over 22-countries, ePubWealth.com is a leader in ePublishing, book promotion, and ebook marketing.

As the creator and author of "The ePubWealth Program," Leland teaches up-and-coming authors the ins-and-outs of today's ePublishing world. He has assisted hundreds of authors make it big in the ePublishing world.

Leland also created a series of external book promotion programs and teaches authors how to promote their books using external marketing sources.

Leland is also the Managing Director of Applied Mind Sciences, the company's mind research unit and Chief Forensics Investigator for the company's ForensicsNation unit. He is active in privacy rights through the company's PrivacyNations unit and is an expert in survival planning and disaster relief through the company's SurvivalNations unit.

Leland resides in Southern Utah.

Visit some of his websites
http://www.AddMeInNow.com
http://www.AppliedMindSciences.com
http://www.BookbuilderPLUS.com
http://www.BookJumping.com
http://www.EmailNations.com
http://www.EmbarrassingProblemsFix.com
http://www.ePubWealth.com
http://www.ForensicsNation.com
http://www.ForensicsNationStore.com
http://www.FreebiesNation.com
http://www.HealthFitnessWellnessNation.com
http://www.Neternatives.com
http://www.PrivacyNations.com
http://www.RetireWithoutMoney.org
http://www.SurvivalNations.com
http://www.TheBentonKitchen.com
http://www.Theolegions.org
http://www.VideoBookbuilder.com

www.ingramcontent.com/pod-product-compliance
Lightning Source LLC
Chambersburg PA
CBHW051805170526
45167CB00005B/1890

* 9 7 8 1 4 9 6 1 8 3 7 0 5 *